Anti-Inflammatory Diet For Beginners

The Ultimate Guide To Reduce Inflammation And Lose Weight With 2000 Days Of Recipes And 61-Day Meal Plan

By

ROSEMARIE JOAQUIN

Table of Contents

Introduction

An anti-inflammatory food is promoted as a cure to fight inflammation in your body. A common principle is that "inflammation" is forever bad. Though it produces horrible side effects, inflammation is really a healthy reaction by our immune structure. When a foreign intruder enters our body, such as bacteria, allergens, or viruses, or damage occurs, the immune cells act immediately. We might sneeze/cough to relieve the body of the wrong agent. We might feel pain & swelling at the location of a cut/injury to show us to be calm in this fragile area. Blood streams in rapidly, which might produce tenderness or irritation. These are indications that the immune system is repairing broken tissue or battling invaders. As recovery takes place, swelling steadily subsides.

The anti-inflammatory food focuses on nutritious fats, nutrient-heavy foods, complex carbs, legumes & plenty of fruits & vegetables. You will not see processed foods, extra added sugars, processed grains (such as white bread & white flour) or meat (red) more than twice a week. The aim of this nutritious diet is to decrease chronic swelling in your body.

While swelling is a necessary response of our body to severe injury, research indicates that underlying chronic swelling is linked with chronic diseases. For instance, a 2019 study issued in the journal Nature Med says that chronic systemic swelling—the irritation that is throughout our body—is a reason of many illnesses, including cardiovascular illness, diabetes, chronic kidney illness, non-alcoholic oily liver disease, cancers, autoimmune illnesses & neurodegenerative conditions.

You could combat a few of the irritation through lifestyle variations, like getting sufficient sleep, participating in physical activity, reducing your stress & eating diets that have been indicated to lower swelling (& cutting back on those which tend to affect it).

Chapter 1: What Anti-Inflammatory Diet Actually is?

1.1 Inflammation, clarified

When working to realize the connection between chronic inflammation & chronic disease, Shayna, RD, a Certified & Registered Oncology Dietician with Cancer Wellbeing of Piedmont Clinic in Atlanta, Georgia, recommends that it is started by defining the 2 kinds of inflammation: acute & chronic.

Inflammation is every so often confusing because it might seem ambiguous. On the one hand, swelling is a beneficial process, permitting the body's ability to cure itself. Once you have a disease or damage, the immune system distributes white blood cells & chemicals to battle off the virus or repair has broken tissue." This kind of inflammation is known as acute inflammation, & it is beneficial to our bodies.

Inflammation might become serious once it stays, even at minimal levels, for long periods of time. Carolyn, Ph.D. RD, a certified dietitian & author of many anti-inflammatory books, shares, "Chronic swelling is like a tiny fire burning in the body that, over a while, gets stoked & fortified by other irritants, captivating a steady toll on our body by destructive cells, overburdening the immune system & creating an imbalance that could lead to long-period health problems.

Komar agrees, "Once you do not have a disease or injury, swelling can potentially harm healthy tissues. Low-grade irritation is inflammation that never actually resolves. It is the reverse of 'good' inflammation & may actually harm DNA."

This is specifically problematic to those who are undertaking therapy for a chronic illness, as the inherent chronic inflammation possibly fuels the infection.

The encouraging news is that several of these risk aspects for emerging chronic inflammation & chronic disease are in our hands. One of the simplest & most readily available ways that we could reduce infection is through consuming a diet rich in anti-inflammatory diets.

1.2 What is the anti-inflammatory diet?

Komar gives clarity on the responsibility of anti-inflammatory diets, saying, "Specific food components could affect inflammation paths in our body." She resonates with Williams' statement & shares, "It is just like a small fire: What you consume could either put 'fuel' to that fire by eating several foods that trigger inflammation, or you could stop that fire by subsequent an anti-inflammatory food & lifestyle."

The anti-inflammatory food takes values from Mediterranean food, studied in the late 1960s, & the DASH food (Dietary Methods to Prevent Hypertension), settled in the 1990s, & has been credited to Andrew, MD, Harvard University alumnus & initiator of the Center for Integrative Med at the Arizona University. Weil initiated the anti-inflammatory food, including an anti-inflammatory diet pyramid.

1.3 Basic principles of the anti-inflammatory food

Although the anti-inflammatory food is not a calorie-restricted diet, its emphasis on entire, unprocessed foods & reduced sugars & flours might cause weight loss.

The rules suggest eating between 2k to 3k calories every day, varying on gender & activity level, with men & more active people requiring more calories, & women & less active people requiring fewer calories.

The anti-inflammatory food advises that 40 to 50 % of everyday calories come from carbs, 30 % from fat & 20 to 30 % from protein, with a highlighting on including carbs, fat, & protein in every single meal.

Carbs

Vegetables & fruits shall make up most of the carbs eaten every day on the anti-inflammatory food. Beans & whole grains (not entire wheat flour) could also be eaten to add bulk & satiety to this classification.

Fats

Monounsaturated fats such as additional-virgin olive oil, avocados, seeds, & nuts are the nutritious fats to be had on anti-inflammatory food. Saturated fats, involving animal fats

& fats that are strong at room temperature, must be used carefully. Polyunsaturated fats involve omega-6 & omega-3 fatty acids & fats that stay liquid at room temp; focus on involving omega-3 fatty acids from this classification.

Proteins

A highlighting on plant-based & lean protein is advised on the anti-inflammatory food. Beans, especially soybeans & whole soy products, & fish, particularly fish rich in omega-3 fatty acids, are advised. Restrict animal protein & prevent red meat.

Adding on, the anti-inflammatory food suggests that the scheduling of your meals is crucial. Dr. Weil advises that calories be ingested within an eleven-hour window, dropping thirteen hours during the night as a "fasting period." He recommends that this fasting period offers time for your body to recalibrate resistance, repair cells, & replenish its capability for antioxidants.

1.4 Five kinds of anti-inflammatory foodstuffs to eat

It is significant to look at the whole diet you eat instead of concentrating on individual diets. Komar urges her clients to look at diet as a component of their treatment strategy.

Research shows that by reliably focusing on a nutritious diet pattern, you could reduce swelling. Komar shares, "It's all about concentrating on the pattern of consuming as opposed to selecting a few specific foods to decrease inflammation."

With this thing in mind, let's look at five kinds of foods vital to anti-inflammatory food, & the properties of each that are supported by studies & by specialists in this field.

Vegetables, particularly cruciferous vegetables

Vegetables offer nutrients that are crucial to fighting to swell & maintaining proper body purpose. Packed with vitamins & minerals, vegetables are also an excellent source of fiber.

Cabbage, broccoli, kale, Brussels sprouts, collard, cauliflower, arugula, greens, & even wasabi are just some of the types in a crew of plants called cruciferous veggies. These vegetables are identifiable for their bitter smell and sometimes sour flavor & are often hyped for their anti-cancer capabilities. These nutrient-rich vegetables contain carotenoids, a kind of antioxidant, vitamins E, K, and C, folate, minerals, & fiber.

Fibrous foods, particularly legumes

A clip of the Mediterranean & anti-inflammatory food, legumes are a kind of vegetable that contains beans, peas, & lentils. Legumes offer some of the maximum natural supplies of fiber discovered in any food & also provide an exceptional basis for plant-based protein.

Fiber is crucial to lowering inflammation, & the intake of legumes has been indicated to have an effect on the body's immune role. A food high in fiber has yet to be discovered to protect against specific cancers, as well as breast cancer.

Fruit particularly berries

Fruit is nature's sweet. Whereas processed sugar is inflammatory & should be prevented on anti-inflammatory food, fruit is anti-inflammatory. It aids in offering much-required energy by offering a raise of natural sugar & you do not get the sugar crush of a refined sugar item because fruit includes fiber, which reduces down the metabolic method & stabilizes blood sugar.

Of all the lovely fruits offered to us, berries are the best of show to decrease inflammation. Blueberries, blackberries, raspberries and strawberries are rich in antioxidants & are just some of the several berries that are recommended as a component of an anti-inflammatory food. Furthermore, the anthocyanins that generate berries' beautiful shades are also potent phytochemicals that might provide anti-inflammatory properties.

Herbs & Spices, particularly turmeric, ginger, cinnamon, & garlic

Frequently overlooked as a supply of nutrition, herbs & spices provide exceptional anti-inflammatory abilities. In addition to consuming a wide variety of vegetables & fruits, Komar shares, "It's also crucial to combine herbs & spices such as turmeric, ginger, cinnamon, and garlic to help reduce inflammation."

- Turmeric is a main resource of curcumin, a micro-nutrient that has been well-known for its antioxidant & anti-inflammatory abilities. When combining turmeric to recipes, additionally add a touch of black pepper to enhance the assimilation of curcumin.

- Ginger is a root that could reduce inflammation & pain, making it tremendously helpful to those occupied to decrease chronic inflammation. Research has also found that ingesting ginger helps relieve nausea & vomiting that several patients feel during chemotherapy therapies for cancer.

- Cinnamon is a flavor that has been frequently used since 2800 BC. It is being examined for its possibility in cancer therapy & has been indicated to have antioxidant & anti-inflammatory abilities.

- Garlic is not just a mouthwatering way to combine a depth of flavor to the dishes. It is a rich resource of selenium with sulfur-comprising compounds, which are being explored for their potential effect on pollutants.

Lean protein, particularly fish

Protein is essential to the creation, maintenance, & restoration of body tissues. Making sure that you get a sufficient quantity of protein in the daily diet is particularly significant as we get older in order to sustain muscle mass.

In addition to being an exceptional resource of lean protein, fish is also high in omega-3 fatty acids, which are essential to reducing inflammation. Fatty seafood like salmon, albacore tuna, trout, Atlantic mackerel, sardines, Atlantic herring, anchovies, & even mussels, offers an excellent nutritional source of omega-threes & lean protein.

1.5 Inflammatory foods to limit

It is characteristically best to embrace a positive approach of incorporating as much anti-inflammatories and entire foods as feasible in the diet to clear out the inflammatory diets. But it is also useful to recognize the foodstuffs which are the biggest donors to inflammation and restrict them in the everyday diet.

Refined sugars

Natural sugars discovered in fruit are not incendiary in nature. Though, when we see refined sugars, the narrative is not the same. Refined sugars contain cane sugar, powdered sugar, brown sugar, granulated sugar, Rich fructose corn syrup and the list goes on.

With no nutrients/fiber to reduce the absorption activity, these products provide slightly to no nutritional value, & ingestion of refined sugars has been linked with enhanced inflammation leading to greater instances of heart disease, cancer, and cognitive and diabetes decline. Look at brands. When purchasing packed foods, manufacturers frequently sneak in extra sugar to make foods more shelf-stable.

Processed & ultra-processed diets

The more a diet converts from its new source before you consume it, the more expected it is to trigger inflammation. A latest study discovered that higher consumption of ultra-processed diets was linked with a greater risk of inflammatory bowel infection.

The majority of packed foods, fast foods, & industrially created items are processed/ultra-processed. Prevent the most awful of these by reading brands & choosing diets with the lowest no of ingredients (items you know & can pronounce & that don't include extra sugar).

Furthermore, there is a connection between ultra-processed foods & sugars: Ultra-processed diets make up 90 percent of the extra sugars Americans eat. If you drop out of the ultra-processed diets, you go a prolonged way in dropping out the extra sugar.

Refined grains

While entire grains are suggested for their anti-inflammatory capabilities, research indicates that the consumption of refined grains is linked with pro-inflammatory causes.

Prevent foods or supplies made with flour, white rice, & pasta & scan brands for the term "enriched." If a food article has been "enhanced," it indicates that nutrients were carried out in processing & then added back in throughout production. This indicates a refined grain effect & should be prevented.

Trans fats

These fats are oils that have been changed chemically during processing & studies suggest that they're directly connected to systemic irritation in women.

Fast foods, packaged snacks, shortening, bakery goods, fried foods, & margarine are popular sources of trans fats. Furthermore, packed foods with ingredients indicated as "hydrogenated"/"partially-hydrogenated" are signs that the diet includes trans fats.

1.6 The Research So Far

Most accessible research focuses on diets & dietary patterns that are linked with metaflammation, that in turn improves to the determination of the elements of an anti-inflammatory food. Metaflammation is especially linked with Western-type nutritional patterns rich in processed meats, refined sugars, salt, saturated fat, & white flour while staying low in fiber, nutrients, & phytochemicals. These foods also be likely to be calorie-concentrated with a rich glycemic load, possibly leading to blood sugar rises, insulin resistance, & excess weight increase. Surveys have indicated that Western foods are linked with enhanced blood markers of swelling, though the association might be due to a sequence of events instead of one direct act. For example, the experience of air pollution & chronic mental anxiety could lead to an extra of free radicals generated in your body, which then oxidize & damage other particles. Atherosclerosis is a situation in which these available radicals corrode LDL cholesterol elements. The acts of both dissolved LDL cholesterol & several kinds of immune cells form wounds & plaque in the heart veins that could lead to ischemic heart illness (a kind of heart illness caused by tightened or partly blocked arteries). Long-term nutrition that is rich in saturated fat & cholesterol might raise LDL levels, raising the risk of the available radical act that might promote this immune reaction, which partly promotes to a persistent low-level pro-inflammatory condition.

The main cause of low-level irritation is the development of fatty acids in the fat tissue (& other tissues) endorsed by a rich-fat or rich-sugar diet. This might cause fat tissue to transmit signals to your immune cells that generate inflammation in numerous areas,

including tissues such as the pancreas. An irritated pancreas could then lead to insulin endurance & diabetes. Therefore, the mixture of holding extra body fat (overweightness) & eating a diet rich in saturated fat & refined sugars improves the risk of cell destruction because of improved immune cell action.

An anti-inflammatory food contains foods high in nutrients, fiber, & phytochemicals & limits foods discovered in a standard Western diet to assist in reducing oxidative stress & inflammation. There is similarly emerging research examining the effects of rich-fiber plant-high diets that maintain a greater variety of beneficial gut microorganisms, which might prevent a situation known as metabolic endotoxemia. It is a low-grade swelling that happens because of a rise in the no of endotoxins that are believed to trigger the inflammation linked with metabolic illnesses like cardiovascular disease & type 2 diabetes.

- A randomized examination of contributors at risk for cardiac disease discovered that Mediterranean food with importance on fresh fruits, legumes, vegetables, nuts, seafood, & olive oil drastically decreased various markers of irritation associated with low-fat food.

- There are presently no standardized nutritional guidelines for rheumatic arthritis, an autoimmune illness that triggers inflammation of joints & breakdown of bone & cartilage. A vegetarian diet, Mediterranean intake, & elimination diet (preventing specific foodstuff allergens) have been indicated in some findings to suppress pro-inflammatory cells & improve symptoms in individuals with rheumatoid arthritis. Individuals tend to describe worse signs when eating specific diets like red meat, alcohol, & soda, whereas fish & berries are stated to improve signs. The Anti-inflammatory Food In Rheumatic Arthritis randomized regulated crossover examination analyzed individuals with rheumatic arthritis who were designated to either a food with anti-inflammatory diets or a control food for ten weeks. After a four-month washout time, the contributors switched foods. The research found that the illness activity score substantially decreased throughout the anti-inflammatory food intervention period.

- Vegetarian foods are based on huge quantities of whole grains, nuts, legumes, & fruits and vegetables. A meta-analysis of seventeen experimental cross-sectional studies discovered that following a vegan diet (including vegetarian foods with no animal diets & lacto-ovo-vegan diets with eggs & dairy) for at slightest years was linked with lesser C-reactive protein points, a pro-inflammatory indicator, than in humans who had no nutritional restrictions.

- The MIND food, a fusion of the DASH & Mediterranean foods, is an anti-inflammatory consumption plan that contains whole grains, veggies, particularly green leafy kinds, berries, beans, nuts, olive oil fish & poultry, & limits fried or fast food, butter, sweets, red meat, and cheese. The MIND food was discovered to significantly decrease the prevalence of Alzheimer's illness, a chronic pro-inflammatory state, in a group of 923 elder adults. Those who trailed the food the most carefully showed a 53 percent decreased rate of the illness, but even individuals who followed the food intake fairly had a 35 percent reduced amount.

- Two separate studies following three large groups (Nurses' Health Study I & II & the Health Specialists Follow-up Research) rated the contributors' foods using a nutritional inflammatory pattern count. These scores were specified based on concentrations of several incendiary markers in our body involving C-reactive protein. Incendiary foods comprised of red, processed, & organ meats; processed carbs; & sweetened beverages. Anti-inflammatory foods included green leafy & dark yellow veggies, whole grains, fruit, tea, & coffee. The studies discovered that when evaluating participants with the maximum to minimum inflammatory food scores, the maximum scores were linked with an enhanced risk of cardiac disease & twice the danger of type two diabetes.

- Large group studies following men & women in the Well-being Professionals Follow-up Study & Nurses Health Studies discovered an improved risk of Crohn's disease & colorectal cancer in individuals who consumed diets highest in incendiary foods. A certified score known as the Empirical Dietary Inflammatory Pattern (EDIP) was established that evaluated markers of swelling in the blood like C-reactive protein & tumor necrosis caused by consuming certain diets. A high EDIP count showed a proinflammatory food intake, which was linked with higher consumption of overall calories, red meat, processed grains, & soda. Lesser scores showed an anti-inflammatory food, which was linked with the consumption of leafy green veggies, dark yellow veggies, coffee, & tea.

Inflammation & the leaky gut

Although the field of study is relatively new, accumulating evidence points to a link between numerous disorders and diseases & our microbiome. Inflammatory situations like inflammatory arthritis, Hashimoto thyroiditis, celiac illness, Crohn's illness, chronic overweightness, & non-alcoholic liver failure have been linked to elevated levels of bacteria in parts of the body where they shouldn't be, a condition known as dysbiosis, and increased gut permeability, also known as "leaky gut." A sheet of epithelial cells that form a tight junction barrier lines the large and small intestines of our digestive tract, preventing bacterial transfer. Bacterial translocation happens when pathogens from the gut—along with viruses, allergens, and pollens into the circulation and other parts of the body. Translocation may result in inflammation or illness. By signaling immune cells, this gut barrier also controls some immunological processes. In the gut, there are naturally occurring beneficial bacteria. If there are any abnormal variations in the quantity or type of these bacteria (for instance, as a result of chronic strain or the consumption of antibiotics/non-steroidal anti-inflammatory drugs), this can alter the intestinal barrier, reducing the body's immune defenses and raising the risk of illness. There is some debate as to whether the sickness or inflammation caused by a leaky gut causes dysbiosis or vice versa.

The use of drugs and toxins in the diet is the most causative factor of leaky gut (for instance, gluten acts as a pollutant in susceptible individuals with celiac disease). Clinical studies have shown that some foods, like the amino acids glutamate and tryptophan, may improve tight junctions & reduce intestinal permeability. The addition of fiber to the diet may enhance the variety of gut bacteria, that in turn boosts the synthesis of narrow fatty acids as well as other healthy metabolites and improves the intestinal barrier. Studies

are also being done on probiotic supplements & foods that are high in prebiotics & probiotics. The connection among dysbiosis or inflammatory disorders, as well as possible therapies, still needs much more study.

Possible Mistakes

- The anti-inflammatory food is adaptable since it doesn't call for following set food patterns. However, doing so necessitates finding recipes that use the plan's ingredients and making one's meal plans.

- Calorie levels & portion sizes aren't underlined in this plan. Thus it is easy to put on weight if enormous quantities are taken.

- People who are unfamiliar with meal planning or preparation may require more detailed advice.

Chapter 2: Breakfast Recipes

2.1   Egg Scramble and Spinach along with Raspberries

Preparation Time: 5 mins

Cooking Time: 10 mins

Servings: 2

Ingredients

- Canola oil, 1 tsp

- Baby spinach, 1 1/2 ounces

- Lightly beaten eggs, 2

- Kosher salt, pinch

- Ground pepper, pinch

- Toasted bread (whole-grain), 1 slice

- Fresh raspberries, ½ cup

Steps

1. On med heat, put the oil in the nonstick skillet. Put spinach & cook for around two mins till it's wilted, whisking often. On the plate, put the spinach. Clean the skillet & put it on med heat & then add the eggs. Cook for around two mins, whisking once/twice. Whisk in the salt, pepper & spinach. Eat the scramble with raspberries & toast.

Nutritional Serving

296 Cal, Protein: 17.8g, Carb: 20.9g, Fat 15.7g

2.2 Southwestern Waffle

Preparation Time: 5 mins

Cooking Time: 8 mins

Servings: 1

Ingredients

- Frozen waffle (whole-grain), 1

- Cooked egg, 1

- Peeled & minced avocado (seeded), ¼ med

- Fresh salsa, 1 tbsp

Steps

1. As per the package instruction, Toast the waffle. Top with avocado, salsa & egg.

Nutritional Serving

207 Cal, Protein: 9g, Carb: 17g, Fat 12g

2.3 Egg Salad, Avocado Toast

Preparation Time: 5 mins

Cooking Time: 5 mins

Servings: 1

Ingredients

- Avocado, 1/4

- Celery, 1 tbsp

- Lemon juice, 1/2 tsp

- Hot sauce, 1/2 tsp

- Salt, Pinch

- Minced hardboiled egg, 1

- Toast (whole-wheat), 1 slice

Steps

1. With the lemon juice, celery, hot sauce & salt, mash the avocado in the bowl. Combine the hard-boiled egg in the same bowl. Scatter on toast.

Nutritional Serving

230 Cal, Protein: 10.9g, Carb: 17.2g, Fat 13.7g

2.4 Cream Cheese Omelet and Smoked Salmon

Preparation Time: 5 mins

Cooking Time: 10 mins

Servings: 1

Ingredients

- Eggs, 2

- Low-fat milk, 1 tsp

- Ground pepper, 1/8 tsp

- Salt, Pinch

- Butter, 1 tsp

- Minced smoked salmon, 2 tbsp

- Softened cream cheese, 1 tbsp

- Thinly minced red onion, 1 tbsp
- Minced fresh dill, 1 ½ tsp

Steps

1. In the bowl, stir the milk, eggs, salt & pepper.

2. In the nonstick skillet, melt the butter on med heat, tilting the skillet to ensure that the whole bottom is coated. Put the egg combination & cook for around one minute without whisking. On one-half of the eggs, drizzle the cheese, salmon, onion & dill. Now cook for around one minute. Use the flexible spatula to lift the bare side to allow the raw egg from the center to flow underneath. It might be necessary to slightly tilt the skillet. Up until there is hardly any uncooked egg on top, keep lifting in various spots. 2 more mins of cooking.

3. Fold the omelet in half and then use the spatula to turn the bare side on the filling. Cook for one minute. (turn the heat down if the eggs are beginning to brown.) After carefully turning it over, heat it for another minute. Serve right now and top with additional dill & pepper, if preferred.

Nutritional Serving

206 Cal, Protein: 16.9g, Carb: 2.7g, Fat 8.6g

2.5 Green Smoothie

Preparation Time: 5 mins

Cooking Time: 5 mins

Servings: 1

Ingredients

- Ripe banana, 1
- Coarsely minced mature kale/ packed baby kale, 1 cup
- Vanilla almond milk (unsweetened), 1 cup
- Ripe avocado, 1/4

- Chia seeds, 1 tbsp

- Honey, 2 tsp

- Ice cubes, 1 cup

Steps

1. In the food processor, Mix the kale, banana, avocado, almond milk, honey & chia seeds. Blend till smooth & creamy. Put in ice & blend till it's smooth.

Nutritional Serving

212 Cal, Protein: 5.9g, Carb: 54.7g, Fat 14.2g

2.6 Kale Omelet and Avocado

Preparation Time: 6 mins

Cooking Time: 10 mins

Servings: 1

Ingredients

- Eggs, 2

- Reduce-fat milk, 1 tsp

- Salt, Pinch

- Olive oil(extra-virgin), 2 tsp

- Minced kale, 1 cup

- Lime juice, 1 tbsp

- Minced fresh coriander, 1 tbsp

- Sunflower seeds (unsalted), 1 tsp

- Salt, Pinch

- Crushed red pepper, pinch

- Sliced avocado, 1/4

Steps

1. With milk & salt, Beat the eggs in the bowl. In the nonstick skillet, Heat the one tsp oil on med heat. Put the egg combination & cook for around two mins till the bottom is ready & the middle is still a little runny. Turn the omelet over & cook for around 30 seconds till it's set. Now move it to the plate.

2. Toss the kale with leftover 1 tsp oil, coriander, lime juice, crushed red pepper, a Pinch of salt & sunflower seeds. Now with the avocado & kale salad, Top the omelet.

Nutritional Serving

312 Cal, Protein: 15g, Carb: 8.6g, Fat 28.1g

2.7 Mango & Kale Smoothie

Preparation Time: 7 mins

Cooking Time: 9 mins

Servings: 1

Ingredients

- baby kale, 1 cup

- mango chunks (frozen), 1 cup

- sliced banana, 1

- orange juice (fresh), 1 cup

Steps

1. In the blender, put the kale, banana, orange juice & mango. Process it on med speed till well mixed.

2. Now Increase the speed to high & process till it's very smooth.

Nutritional Serving

323 Cal, Protein: 3g, Carb: 49g, Fat 1g

2.8 Salad For Breakfast with Salsa Verde Vinaigrette and Egg

Preparation Time: 5 mins

Cooking Time: 10 mins

Servings: 1

Ingredients

- Salsa verde, 3 tbsp

- Olive oil (extra-virgin), 1 tbsp + 1 tsp

- Minced coriander, 2 tbsp

- Mesclun, 2 cups

- Broken blue corn tortilla chips in big pieces, 8

- Rinsed red kidney beans(canned), ½ cup

- Sliced avocado, ¼

- Egg, 1

Steps

1. In the bowl, Stir 1 Tbsp oil, coriander & salsa. With mesclun, Toss half of the combination in the dinner bowl.

2. Layer beans, avocado & chips on top of the salad.

3. Put the leftover 1 tsp oil in the nonstick pan on med heat. Put egg & fry for around two mins till the white is fully cooked while the yolk is a little bit runny.

4. On the salad, Serve the egg. Sprinkle with a leftover salsa vinaigrette & drizzle with more coriander, if needed.

Nutritional Serving

412 Cal, Protein: 4g, Carb: 82g, Fat 1g

2.9 Smoothie of Cherry Mocha

Preparation Time: 10 mins

Cooking Time: 10 mins

Servings: 2

Ingredients

- Unsweetened & frozen pitted dark sweet cherries, 1 cup
- Chocolate flavor almond milk(unsweetened), 1 cup
- Fat-free carton of vanilla greek yogurt, 6 ounces
- Banana, 1/2
- Cocoa powder(unsweetened), 2 tbsp
- Almond butter, 2 tbsp
- Coffee powder(instant espresso), 1 tsp
- Vanilla, 1 tsp
- Ice cubes, 2 cups
- Espresso beans(chocolate-covered), 1 tbsp

Steps

1. Put the almond milk, cherries, banana, Greek yogurt, almond butter, cocoa powder, vanilla & espresso coffee powder In the blender. Cover it & process it till smooth. Put in the ice cubes; Cover & process till smooth. Put into glasses & if needed, garnish with espresso beans(chocolate-covered) & further banana slices.

Nutritional Serving

300 Cal, Protein: 13g, Carb: 34g, Fat 12g

2.10 Avocado Toast (West Coast)

Preparation Time: 8 mins

Cooking Time: 8 mins

Servings: 1

Ingredients

- Combined salad greens, 1 cup

- Red-wine vinegar, 1 tsp

- Olive oil(extra-virgin), 1 tsp

- Pepper, Pinch

- Salt, Pinch

- Toasted sprouted bread(whole-wheat), 2 slices

- Plain hummus, ¼ cup

- Alfalfa sprouts, ¼ cup

- Sliced avocado, ¼

- Sunflower seeds(unsalted), 2 tsp

Steps

1. In the med bowl, Toss the greens with oil, vinegar, pepper & salt. With 2 tbsp of hummus, scatter every toast slice. Garnish with avocado, greens & sprouts & then drizzle the sunflower seeds.

Nutritional Serving

412 Cal, Protein: 16.2g, Carb: 46.4g, Fat 21.9g

2.11 Smoothie of Strawberry-Almond

Preparation Time: 5 mins

Cooking Time: 8 mins

Servings: 2

Ingredients

- Strawberries(frozen), 10

- Almond milk, 1 cup

- Silken tofu, 1/2 cup

- Sugar, 2 tbsp

Steps

1. In a blender, put the almond milk, strawberries, sugar & tofu. Process for one min till smooth & frothy. Put it into the tall glasses & serve.

Nutritional Serving

312 Cal, Protein: 4.6g, Carb: 30.4g, Fat 3.3g

2.12 Feta and Spinach Scrambled Egg Pitas

Preparation Time: 10 mins

Cooking Time: 15 mins

Servings: 4

Ingredients

- Olive oil(extra-virgin), 1 tbsp

- Block frozen minced spinach(thawed & drained), 10 ounces

- Salt, Pinch

- Beaten eggs, 8

- Thinly crushed feta cheese

- Ground pepper, Pinch

- Tomato pesto(sun-dried)/tomato tapenade(sun-dried), 8 tsp

- Sliced in half pitas (whole-wheat, 4

Steps

1. In a large nonstick skillet, put the oil on med heat. Put salt & spinach, then cook till it's steaming hot, whisking rarely. Put eggs & cook for around five mins, whisking the eggs till they are moist & become soft. Put pepper & feta, then cook till set.

2. Scatter the pesto/tapenade inside the pita pockets, two tsp/ pita. Split the egg combination between the pitas.

Nutritional Serving

303 Cal, Protein: 19.9g, Carb: 21.1g, Fat 16.2g

2.13 Avocado and Blueberry Smoothie

Preparation Time: 8 mins

Cooking Time: 10 mins

Servings: 1

Ingredients

- Frozen blueberries, 1 cup

- Pitted & sliced avocado, ½

- Pitted & roughly minced dates, 5

- Vanilla coconut milk(unsweetened), 1 cup

Steps

1. In the blender, put the avocado, blueberries, coconut milk & dates. Process it on med speed till well combined; use the tamper if required.

2. Increase the blender's speed to high & process till it's smooth.

Nutritional Serving

405 Cal, Protein: 4g, Carb: 59g, Fat 20g

2.14 Breakfast Salad of Baby Kale with Avocado and Smoked Trout

Preparation Time: 5 mins

Cooking Time: 10 mins

Servings: 1

Ingredients

- Chopped garlic, 1 tsp

- Salt, Pinch

- Olive oil(extra-virgin), 1 tbsp

- Red-wine vinegar, 2 tsp

- Pepper, Pinch

- Baby kale(lightly packed), 3 cups

- Flaked smoked trout, ¼ cup

- Diced avocado(firm ripe), ¼

- Thinly minced red onion, 1 tbsp

Steps

1. To make the paste, Mash the garlic & salt with the chef's knife side. Stir the oil, garlic paste, pepper & vinegar together in the bowl. Put kale. Toss to cover. Top with avocado, red onion & trout. Now serve it.

Nutritional Serving

275 Cal, Protein: 10.1g, Carb: 9.4g, Fat 23g

2.15 Arugula and Avocado Omelet

Preparation Time: 10 mins

Cooking Time: 10 mins

Servings: 1

Ingredients

- Eggs, 2
- Reduce-fat milk, 1 tsp
- Salt, ⅛ tsp
- Olive oil(extra-virgin), 2 tsp
- Arugula, ½ cup
- Lemon juice, 1 tsp
- Diced avocado, ¼
- Plain Greek yogurt(whole-milk), 2 tbsp

Steps

1. In the bowl, Stir the eggs with the salt pinch & milk. In the nonstick pan, put 1 tsp oil on med heat. Put the egg combination & cook for around two mins till the bottom is ready & the middle is a little runny. Turn the omelet & cook for further 30 seconds. Now move it to the plate.

2. In the bowl, Toss the arugula with leftover 1 tsp oil & lemon juice. Garnish the omelet with yogurt, arugula, a Pinch of salt & avocado.

Nutritional Serving

344 Cal, Protein: 16.9g, Carb: 7.2g, Fat 28g

2.16 Spinach Smoothie

Preparation Time: 7 mins

Cooking Time: 10 mins

Servings: 1

Ingredients

- Baby spinach, 1 ½ cups
- Sliced banana, 1

- Frozen strawberries, 1 cup

- Vanilla coconut milk(unsweetened), 2/3 cup

Steps

1. In the blender, put the banana, spinach, coconut milk & strawberries. Process it on med speed till well combined.

2. Then Increase the speed to high & process till it's smooth.

Nutritional Serving

183 Cal, Protein: 4g, Carb: 39g, Fat 4g

2.17 Spinach Scrambled Eggs and Smoked Trout

Preparation Time: 10 mins

Cooking Time: 10 mins

Servings: 2

Ingredients

- Eggs, 4

- Low-fat milk, 2 tbsp

- Ground pepper, ¼ tsp

- Salt, Pinch

- Grapeseed oil/avocado oil, 2 tsp

- Thinly minced shallot, 2 tbsp

- Flaked & boned smoked trout, ½ cup

- Minced spinach, 1 cup

Steps

1. In the bowl, put the milk, eggs, salt & pepper. Then stir till it's fully pale yellow.

2. In the nonstick pan, put the oil on med heat. Put shallot & cook for around two mins, whisking, till it's beginning to brown. Put in the egg combination & lower the heat. Cook for around thirty seconds till the edges are set. Drizzle trout on the eggs. Use the rubber spatula to nicely fold & push the eggs till it's fluffy & just set; it will take around 3 mins. Whisk in the spinach. Take it from heat, Cover, & set aside for around 2 minutes or till the spinach is barely wilted.

Nutritional Serving

243 Cal, Protein: 19g, Carb: 3.9g, Fat 16.7g

2.18 Smoothie Bowl of Mango-Almond

Preparation Time: 5 mins

Cooking Time: 10 mins

Servings: 1

Ingredients

- Frozen minced mango, ½ cup

- Plain Greek yogurt(nonfat), ½ cup

- Frozen sliced banana, ¼ cup

- Plain almond milk(unsweetened), ¼ cup

- Unsalted almonds, 5 tbsp

- Ground allspice, ⅛ tsp

- Raspberries, ¼ cup

- Honey, ½ tsp

Steps

1. In the blender, put yogurt, mango, almond milk, banana, 3 tbsp almonds & allspice. Process till it's very smooth.

2. In the bowl, put the smoothie & garnish with leftover 2 tbsp almonds, honey & raspberries.

Nutritional Serving

457 Cal, Protein: 21.6g, Carb: 45.8g, Fat 24.1g

2.19 Breakfast Beans with the Microwave Poached Egg

Preparation Time: 10 mins

Cooking Time: 15 mins

Servings: 2

Ingredients

- Canola oil, 2 tsp

- Minced red bell pepper, ¼ cup

- Minced scallions, 2

- Ground cumin, ½ tsp

- Reduced sodium black beans(canned), ¾ cup

- Cooked barley, ½ cup

- Vegetable broth/reduced-sodium chicken broth, ½ cup

- Salt, ⅛ tsp

- Hot sauce, ⅛ tsp

- Water, 1 cup

- Distilled white vinegar, 1 tsp

- Eggs, 2

- Grated pepper jack cheese, 2 tbsp

- Sliced avocado, ½

- Coarsely minced fresh coriander, 2 tbsp

Steps

1. In the skillet, put oil on medium heat. Put scallion whites, cumin & bell pepper; cook for around two mins, frequently whisking, till softened. Put the beans, broth, cooked barley, & salt. Cook for around four mins till the liquid is mostly absorbed. Whisk in hot sauce & scallion greens. Split it among two bowls.

2. In the small bowl (microwave-safe), put the 1/2 tsp vinegar & 1/2 cup water. One egg must be carefully cracked into the water & submerged thoroughly. For approximately a minute on high, microwave the egg till the white is set but the yolk is still a little liquid. With the slotted spoon, remove the egg, pat it dry, and then add it to the bean combination in one dish. Do it again with the leftover egg, 1/2 tsp. Vinegar, & 1/2 cup water.

3. Garnish every bowl with 1/4 avocado & 1 tbsp cheese. Then drizzle with coriander, if needed.

Nutritional Serving

364 Cal, Protein: 16g, Carb: 32g, Fat 20g

2.20 Pineapple and Kale Smoothie

Preparation Time: 6 mins

Cooking Time: 10 mins

Servings: 1

Ingredients

- Baby kale, 1 cup

- Coconut Greek yogurt, ¼ cup

- Pineapple chunks(frozen), 1 cup

- Vanilla coconut milk(unsweetened), ½ cup

- Fresh orange juice, ½ cup

Steps

1. In the blender, put yogurt, kale, coconut milk, orange juice & pineapple. Process it on med speed till well mixed.

2. Then Increase the speed to high & process till it's smooth.

Nutritional Serving

213 Cal, Protein: 9g, Carb: 41g, Fat 3g

2.21 Smoked Salmon Omelet and Avocado

Preparation Time: 8 mins

Cooking Time: 8 mins

Servings: 1

Ingredients

- Eggs, 2

- Reduced-fat milk, 1 tsp

- Salt, Pinch

- Olive oil(extra-virgin), 1 tsp + 1/2 tsp

- Sliced avocado, ¼

- Smoked salmon, 1 ounce

- Minced fresh basil, 1 tbsp

Steps

1. In the bowl, Beat the eggs with salt & milk. In the nonstick skillet, put 1 tsp oil on med heat. Put the egg combination & cook for around two mins till the bottom is ready & the middle is a little runny. Turn the omelet & cook for a further thirty seconds till it's set. Move it to the plate. Garnish with salmon, basil & avocado. Sprinkle with the leftover 1/2 tsp oil.

Nutritional Serving

323 Cal, Protein: 19g, Carb: 5.3g, Fat 25.2g

2.22 Smoothie of Spinach and Avocado

Preparation Time: 5 mins

Cooking Time: 5 mins

Servings: 1

Ingredients

- Plain yogurt(nonfat), 1 cup

- Fresh spinach, 1 cup

- Frozen banana, 1

- Avocado, ¼

- Water, 2 tbsp

- Honey, 1 tsp

Steps

1. In the blender, put spinach, yogurt, avocado, banana, honey & water. Process till smooth.

Nutritional Serving

357 Cal, Protein: 17.7g, Carb: 57.8g, Fat 8.2g

2.23 Toast of Avocado-Egg

Preparation Time: 6 mins

Cooking Time: 8 mins

Servings: 1

Ingredients

- Avocado, ¼

- Ground pepper, ¼ tsp

- Garlic powder, ⅛ tsp

- Toasted bread(whole-wheat), 1 slice

- Fried egg, 1

- Sriracha & sliced scallion, 1 tsp

Steps

1. In the bowl, Combine pepper, garlic powder & avocado, then gently mash.

2. Garnish the toast with the fried egg & avocado combination. Top with scallion & Sriracha, if you like.

Nutritional Serving

271 Cal, Protein: 11.5g, Carb: 18.1g, Fat 17.7g

2.24 Spinach and Kale Smoothie

Preparation Time: 5 mins

Cooking Time: 10 mins

Servings: 1

Ingredients

- Baby kale, 1 cup

- Baby spinach, 1 cup

- Pitted & roughly minced dates, 5

- Creamy almond butter, 2 tbsp

- Peeled & sliced kiwi, 1

- Vanilla almond milk(unsweetened), 1 cup

Steps

1. In the blender, Put spinach, kale, kiwi, dates, almond milk & almond butter. Process it on med speed till well combined.

2. Then Increase the speed to high & process till it's smooth.

Nutritional Serving

419 Cal, Protein: 12g, Carb: 51g, Fat 21g

2.25 Smoked Salmon Scrambled Eggs

Preparation Time: 9 mins

Cooking Time: 11 mins

Servings: 1

Ingredients

- Eggs, 2

- Minced smoked salmon, 1 ounce

- Low-fat cream cheese, 2 tsp

- Sliced scallion, 1

- Rinsed capers, 1 tsp

Steps

1. In the bowl, Lightly beat the eggs till mixed. Whisk in cream cheese, smoked salmon, capers & scallion. With cooking spray, Coat the nonstick skillet & heat it on medium. Put the egg combination & cook for around three mins while whisking frequently.

Nutritional Serving

205 Cal, Protein: 18.7g, Carb: 2.3g, Fat 12.8g

Chapter 3: Lunch Recipes

3.1 Tomato, Arugula Salad and Cucumber with Hummus

Preparation Time: 7 mins

Cooking Time: 10 mins

Servings: 1

Ingredients

- Arugula, 2 cups

- Halved cherry tomatoes, ⅓ cup

- Sliced cucumber, ⅓ cup

- Minced red onion, 1 tbsp

- Olive oil(extra-virgin), 1 ½ tbsp

- Red-wine vinegar, 2 tsp

- Ground pepper, ⅛ tsp

- Feta cheese, 1 tbsp

- Whole-wheat pita, 1 4-inch

- Hummus, ¼ cup

Steps

1. In the bowl, Toss the arugula with cucumber, tomatoes, oil, onion, pepper & vinegar. Garnish with feta. Eat with the pita & hummus.

Nutritional Serving

422 Cal, Protein: 10.9g, Carb: 30.5g, Fat 29.9g

3.2 Loaded Cucumber & Avocado Sandwich

Preparation Time: 8 mins

Cooking Time: 10 mins

Servings: 1

Ingredients

- Grated Cheddar cheese(extra-sharp), 3 tbsp

- Ricotta cheese, 2 tbsp

- Thinly sliced chives, 4 tsp

- Lemon juice, 2 tsp

- Ground pepper, Pinch

- Lightly toasted sandwich bread(whole-wheat), 2 slices

- Finely sliced red bell pepper, ¼ cup

- Finely sliced cucumber, 1/3 cup

- Sliced avocado, 1/3

Steps

1. In the bowl, whisk the ricotta, Cheddar, lemon juice, chives, pepper & salt. On every toast slice, scatter half of the mixture with pepper, avocado & cucumber, Layer one slice. After this, garnish with the other slice.

Nutritional Serving

403 Cal, Protein: 17g, Carb: 35g, Fat 23g

3.3 Avocado Tuna Spinach Salad

Preparation Time: 8 mins

Cooking Time: 10 mins

Servings: 1

Ingredients

- Water-packed tuna, 5 ounces

- Diced avocado, ¼ cup

- Cherry tomatoes(halved), ¼ cup

- poppy seed dressing, 1 ½ tbsp

- Minced red onion, 1 tbsp

- Olive oil(extra-virgin), 1 tbsp

- Baby spinach, 2 cups

- Sunflower seeds, 1 tbsp

Steps

1. Mix tuna, tomatoes, avocado, onion, dressing & oil in the bowl. Serve on spinach & drizzle with sunflower seeds.

Nutritional Serving

432 Cal, Protein: 20g, Carb: 17g, Fat 32g

3.4 Mashed Chickpea Salad with Dill & Capers

Preparation Time: 8 mins

Cooking Time: 8 mins

Servings: 4

Ingredients

- Reduced sodium chickpeas, 15 ounces

- Thinly minced celery, 1/3 cup

- Vegan mayonnaise, ¼ cup

- Minced fresh dill, ¼ cup

- Finely minced scallion, 1

- Minced capers, 2 tsp

- Lemon juice, 2 tsp

- Ground pepper, ¼ tsp

Steps

1. In the clean kitchen towel, put the chickpeas. Fold that towel over & nicely rub it to remove any loose skin. Remove the skins; move the chickpeas to the bowl. With the

fork, mash the chickpeas. Put mayonnaise, celery, scallion, dill, lemon juice, pepper & capers; whisk till it's well coated.

Nutritional Serving

186 Cal, Protein: 4.9g, Carb: 16.1g, Fat 11.7g

3.5 Mason Jar Salad with Tuna and Chickpeas

Preparation Time: 5 mins

Cooking Time: 5 mins

Servings: 1

Ingredients

- Minced kale, 3 cups

- Honey-mustard vinaigrette, 2 tbsp

- Pouch tuna in water, 1 2.5-ounce

- Canned chickpeas(rinsed), ½ cup

- Peeled & shredded carrot, 1

Steps

1. In the bowl, Toss the kale & dressing; after this, move it to the one-quart mason jar. Garnish with chickpeas, carrots & tuna. Put the jar's lid & store it in a fridge for up to two days.

2. When ready to serve, put the contents of a jar into a dish and mix to blend the salad components with dressed kale.

Nutritional Serving

430 Cal, Protein: 26.4g, Carb: 30.1g, Fat 22.7g

3.6 Hummus and Veggie Sandwich

Preparation Time: 8 mins

Cooking Time: 11 mins

Servings: 1

Ingredients

- Bread(whole-grain), 2 slices

- Hummus, 3 tbsp

- Mashed avocado, ¼

- Combined salad greens, ½ cup

- Sliced red bell pepper, ¼

- Sliced cucumber, ¼ cup

- Shredded carrot, ¼ cup

Steps

1. With the hummus, scatter one bread slice & with the avocado, scatter the other. Fill a sandwich with bell pepper, greens, carrot & cucumber. Cut it in half & eat.

Nutritional Serving

325 Cal, Protein: 12.8g, Carb: 39.7g, Fat 14.3g.

3.7 Tuna-Spinach Salad (Mediterranean)

Preparation Time: 5 mins

Cooking Time: 7 mins

Servings: 1

Ingredients

- Tahini, 1 ½ tbsp

- Lemon juice, 1 ½ tbsp

- Water, 1 ½ tbsp

- Pitted & minced Kalamata olives, 4

- Chunk light tuna in water, 1 5-ounce

- Feta cheese, 2 tbsp

- Parsley, 2 tbsp

- Baby spinach, 2 cups

- Peeled/sliced orange, 1

Steps

1. In the bowl, stir lemon juice, water & tahini. Put olives, tuna, parsley & feta; whisk to mix. Enjoy the tuna salad on two cups of spinach & with orange on a side.

Nutritional Serving

376 Cal, Protein: 25.7g, Carb: 26.2g, Fat 21g

3.8 Minced Veggie Grain Bowls with the Turmeric Dressing

Preparation Time: 8 mins

Cooking Time: 8 mins

Servings: 4

Ingredients

- Packages of cooked quinoa, 8 ounces

- Container minced veggie mix, 16 ounces

- Can chickpeas, 15.5 ounces

- Salad dressing of creamy turmeric, 1/2 cup

Steps

1. As per the package instruction, Prepare the quinoa. Before assembling the bowls, move them to the shallow bowl to let them cool.

2. Split veggies combination between four single-serving containers. Garnish each with 1/4 quinoa & 1/4 of the chickpeas. Cover the containers & put them in the fridge for up to four days.

3. In all 4 lidded containers, add 2 tbsp of salad dressing & put it in a fridge for up to four days.

4. With the dressing, Toss each bowl. Now you can serve.

Nutritional Serving

248 Cal, Protein: 16.7g, Carb: 23.2g, Fat 17g

3.9 Chickpea Salad Sandwich

Preparation Time: 5 mins

Cooking Time: 7 mins

Servings: 4

Ingredients

- Chickpeas(no-salt), 2 cans

- Olive oil(extra-virgin), 6 tbsp

- Lemon juice, 3 tbsp

- Dijon mustard, 2 tsp

- Garlic powder, ½ tsp

- Thinly minced celery, ½ cup

- Thinly minced fresh dill, ¼ cup

- Salt, ⅛ tsp

- Ground pepper, ⅛ tsp

- Vegan mayonnaise, 4 tbsp

- Toasted bread(whole-grain), 8 slices

- Green lettuce leaves, 4

- Thinly sliced red onion, 4

- Tomato slices, 4

Steps

1. Mix oil, chickpeas, mustard, garlic powder & lemon juice. Use the potato masher/ fork to crush chickpeas till most get mashed while a few are still whole. Whisk in dill, celery, pepper & salt.

2. Scatter one tbsp mayonnaise on one side of each bread. Garnish evenly with onion, tomato, lettuce, & chickpea combination. Top with leftover bread, four slices.

Nutritional Serving

623 Cal, Protein: 18g, Carb: 58g, Fat 35g

3.10 Avocado Toast with Burrata

Preparation Time: 5 mins

Cooking Time: 5 mins

Servings: 1

Ingredients

- Whole-grain toast, 1 slice

- Thinly sliced ripe avocado, ½

- Lemon juice, 1 tsp

- Kosher salt, ⅛ tsp

- Ground pepper, ⅛ tsp

- Mozzarella cheese/burrata, 1 ½ ounce

- Thinly sliced fresh basil, 1 tsp

- Chopped fresh chives, 1 tsp

- Aleppo pepper, pinch

Steps

1. With avocado, Top the toast. Sprinkle the lemon juice & drizzle with pepper & salt. Garnish with mozzarella/burrata, chives, Aleppo pepper & basil.

Nutritional Serving

439 Cal, Protein: 18.3g, Carb: 36.9g, Fat 28.1g

3.11 Minced Salad with Peanut Dressing and Sriracha Tofu

Preparation Time: 7 mins

Cooking Time: 10 mins

Servings: 4

Ingredients

- Kale, broccoli, cabbage salad mix & Brussels sprout, 1 package

- Frozen & thawed shelled edamame, 1 package

- Cubed baked tofu(Sriracha flavored), 2 packages

- Spicy peanut vinaigrette, 1/2 cup

Steps

1. Split the salad combination between four single-serving containers. Garnish every with half a cup of edamame & 1/4 of tofu.

2. In each of the four lidded containers, move two tbsp of vinaigrette & put it in the fridge for up to four days.

3. Cover the salad containers & put them in the fridge for up to four days. Before serving it, Dress with a vinaigrette.

Nutritional Serving

385 Cal, Protein: 16g, Carb: 32g, Fat 25g

3.12 Brussels Sprouts Salad with Crunchy Chickpeas

Preparation Time: 5 mins

Cooking Time: 8 mins

Servings: 4

Ingredients

- Shredded Brussels sprouts, 1 package

- Minced kale, 4 cups

- Tahini Sauce with Garlic & Lemon, 1/2 cup

- Roasted chickpea snacks with salt, 1 cup

- Pitted & quartered avocado, 1

Steps

1. Split the Brussels sprouts & kale between four single-serving containers. Cover & put it in the fridge for up to four days.

2. In each of the four lidded containers, move two tbsp of tahini sauce & put it in the fridge for up to four days.

3. Before serving every salad, Sprinkle with one portion of tahini sauce & toss well to coat. Garnish with 1/4 avocado & 1/4 cup roasted chickpeas.

Nutritional Serving

337 Cal, Protein: 11.9g, Carb: 30.6g, Fat 20.2g

3.13 Egg Salad Lettuce Wraps

Preparation Time: 6 mins

Cooking Time: 7 mins

Servings: 1

Ingredients

- Plain Greek yogurt(nonfat), ¼ cup

- Mayonnaise, 1 tbsp

- Dijon mustard, ½ tsp

- Salt, Pinch

- Ground pepper, pinch

- Hard-boiled eggs, 3

- Minced stalks of celery, 2

- Chopped red onion, 2 tbsp

- Iceberg lettuce leaves, 2

- Minced fresh basil, 1 tbsp

- Carrots(peeled & sliced into sticks), 2

Steps

1. In the bowl, stir mayonnaise, yogurt, salt, pepper & mustard.

2. Remove 1 egg yolk. Mince the leftover eggs & move them to a bowl. Put onion & celery, then whisk to mix. Slice the lettuce leaves in half & double-layer them to create two wraps.

3. Split the egg salad between the wraps & garnish with basil. Eat with the carrot sticks on the side.

Nutritional Serving

436 Cal, Protein: 27g, Carb: 20.9g, Fat 27g

3.14 Greek Kale Salad with Chicken and Quinoa

Preparation Time: 5 mins

Cooking Time: 8 mins

Servings: 2

Ingredients

- Minced kale, 4 cups

- Shredded cooked chicken, 1 ½ cups

- Cooked quinoa, 1 cup

- Sliced grated roasted red peppers, ¼ cup

- Greek salad dressing, ¼ cup

- Crumbled feta cheese, 1 ounce

Steps

1. In the bowl, put chicken, kale, roasted peppers & quinoa. Put the dressing & toss to cover. Garnish with feta if you like.

Nutritional Serving

301 Cal, Protein: 29.8g, Carb: 27.1g, Fat 7.9g

3.15 Quinoa Chickpea Salad along with Red Pepper Hummus Dressing (Roasted)

Preparation Time: 6 mins

Cooking Time: 9 mins

Servings: 1

Ingredients

- Hummus(roasted/original red pepper flavor), 2 tbsp

- Lemon juice, 1 tbsp

- Minced roasted red pepper, 1 tbsp

- Mixed salad greens, 2 cups

- Cooked quinoa, ½ cup

- Chickpeas, ½ cup

- Sunflower seeds(unsalted), 1 tbsp

- Minced fresh parsley, 1 tbsp

- Salt, Pinch

- Ground pepper, pinch

Steps

1. In the dish, whisk lemon juice, red peppers & hummus. Then use water for the appropriate consistency of the dressing.

2. In the bowl, arrange the quinoa, chickpeas & greens. Garnish with parsley, sunflower seeds, pepper & salt. Eat it with dressing.

Nutritional Serving

379 Cal, Protein: 16g, Carb: 58.5g, Fat 10.5g

3.16 Special Arugula Omelet

Preparation Time: 5 mins

Cooking Time: 10 mins

Servings: 1

Ingredients

- Eggs, 2

- Reduced fat milk, 1 tsp

- Salt, ⅛ tsp

- Olive oil(extra-virgin), 2 tsp

- Arugula, ½ cup

- Lemon juice, 1 tsp

- Diced avocado, ¼

- Plain Greek yogurt(whole-milk), 2 tbsp

Steps

1. In the bowl, Beat the eggs with salt, pinch & milk. In the nonstick skillet, put one tsp of oil on med heat. Put the egg combination & cook for around two mins, till the bottom is ready & the middle is a little bit runny. Turn the omelet & cook for further 30 seconds till set. Move to the plate.

2. In a small bowl, Toss arugula with leftover one tsp oil lemon juice. Garnish the omelet with yogurt, avocado, arugula & pinch of salt.

Nutritional Serving

344 Cal, Protein: 16.9g, Carb: 7.2g, Fat 28g

3.17 Sweet and Savory Hummus Plate

Preparation Time: 15 mins

Cooking Time: 45 mins

Servings: 4

Ingredients

Garlic Oil and Poached Garlic

- Water, ¾ cup
- Cloves separate Garlic(unpeeled), 4 heads
- Canola oil, 1 ½ cups
- Olive oil(extra-virgin), ½ cup

Bean Dip

- Minced onion, 1 ½ cups
- Salt, ½ tsp
- cannellini beans, 1 can
- lemon juice, 1 tsp

Sweet and Savory Hummus Plate

- Garlic & White Bean Dip, ¾ cup

- Sugar snap peas/green beans, 1 cup

- Mini bell peppers, 8

- Castelvetrano olives, 20

- Watermelon wedges, 8

- Red grapes, 1 cup

- Crackers(gluten-free), 1 cup

- Salted roasted pepitas, 1/2 cup

- Coconut-date balls, 8

Steps

1. Making garlic oil and poached garlic: In the saucepan, bring the water to a simmer. Put the garlic cloves & whisk to combine after turning off the heat. Allow it to rest for fifty minutes or till the garlic skins become soft & chill enough to handle. Take the skins from the garlic, strain it, then cut off the tough nub at the base of each clove's head.

2. In the saucepan, put the canola oil, olive oil & garlic; carry to a gentle boil on low heat. It may be essential to move the skillet to the burner's edge. Boil for around 45 mins, till the clove's color changes to golden & it gets very soft when pressed. Allow it to cool for around 30 minutes.

3. While saving the oil, move the chilled garlic to a strainer to drain. Garlic should be added to a blender and pureed till smooth, occasionally scraping down the edges. If it gives more than half a cup, you may keep the remainder in the fridge for up to one week.

4. Creating bean dip: in the skillet, Mix half of the stored garlic oil, salt & onion. Cook on med heat for around 8 mins, till the onion gets softened while not browned. Whisk in beans & cook till fully heated, which will take around two mins. Move to the blender, put in lemon juice & process with half garlic puree till smooth. Serve cold/warm.

5. Distribute the items evenly among the four plates. Serve with hard cider, if preferred.

Nutritional Serving

654 Cal, Protein: 13.9g, Carb: 83.7g, Fat 30.3g

3.18 Veggie Salad and White Bean

Preparation Time: 5 mins

Cooking Time: 5 mins

Servings: 1

Ingredients

- Mixed salad greens, 2 cups
- Your preferred veggies, 3/4cup
- Canned white beans, 1/3 cup
- Diced avocado, 1/2
- Red-wine vinegar, 1 tbsp
- Extra-virgin olive oil, 2 tsp
- Kosher salt, 1/4 tsp
- Freshly ground pepper, pinch

Steps

1. In the med bowl, mix veggies, greens, avocado & beans. Sprinkle with oil & vinegar, then season with pepper & salt. Toss to mix & move to the big plate.

Nutritional Serving

360 Cal, Protein: 10.1g, Carb: 29.7g, Fat 24.6g

3.19 Salmon Salad-Loaded Avocado

Preparation Time: 7 mins

Cooking Time: 8 mins

Servings: 1

Ingredients

- Canned salmon, 1/3 cup

- Pesto, 1 tbsp

- Plain Greek yogurt(nonfat), 1 tbsp

- Chopped shallot, 2 tsp

- Avocado, ½

- Baby spinach, 1 cup

- Thin wheat crackers, 5

Steps

1. Mix salmon with yogurt, shallot & pesto. Serve on baby spinach & avocado with the crackers.

Nutritional Serving

377 Cal, Protein: 23g, Carb: 20g, Fat 24.1g

3.20 Vegan Bistro Lunch Box

Preparation Time: 5 mins

Cooking Time: 5 mins

Servings: 1

Ingredients

- Hummus, 1/4 cup

- Whole-wheat pita bread(Sliced into four wedges) , 1/2

- Mixed olives, 2 tbsp

- Persian cucumber, 1

- Sliced red bell pepper, 1/4

- Minced fresh dill, 1/4 tsp

Steps

1. In the four-cup divided coverable container, arrange the hummus, olives, pita, bell peppers & cucumber.

Nutritional Serving

194 Cal, Protein: 7.8g, Carb: 23.4g, Fat 8.7g

3.21 Chickpea Salad and Couscous

Preparation Time: 4 mins

Cooking Time: 5 mins

Servings: 1

Ingredients

- Thinly minced kale, 1 cup
- Cooked couscous(whole-wheat), ¾ cup
- Canned chickpeas, 2/3 cup
- Basil Vinaigrette, 4 tbsp

Steps

1. In the bowl, Combine couscous, kale, dressing & chickpeas. Serve right away or put it in the fridge for up to four days.

Nutritional Serving

481 Cal, Protein: 17.3g, Carb: 67.6g, Fat 16.7g

Chapter 4: Dinner Recipes

4.1 Cauliflower Rice Bowl and Sweet Potato

Preparation Time: 10 mins

Cooking Time: 30 mins

Servings: 4

Ingredients

- Sliced sweet potato into 1/4 inch thick, 1

- Olive oil(extra-virgin), 2 tsp + 2 tbsp

- Salt, 2 pinches + 1/2 tsp

- Ground pepper, ½ tsp

- Orange juice, ¼ cup

- Lime juice, 2 tbsp

- Minced fresh coriander, ½ cup

- Chopped cloves garlic, 3

- Ground cumin, ½ tsp

- Dried oregano, ½ tsp

- Cauliflower florets, 5 cups

- Rinsed black beans, 1 can

- Sliced ripe avocado(firm), 1

- Pico de gallo, ½ cup

Steps

1. Set the oven to 400 degrees Fahrenheit.

2. Sweet potatoes should be mixed with 2 teaspoons of oil, a sprinkle of salt, & 1/4 teaspoon of pepper in the bowl. Put it on the cookie sheet. Roast for ten to fourteen minutes or till tender.

3. Mix lime juice, Orange juice, 1 chopped garlic clove, 1/4 cup cilantro, oregano, and a sprinkle of salt & cumin in the bowl.

4. In a blender, pulse the cauliflower florets in 2 batches till the pieces are the size of rice. The leftover 2 tbsp of oil should be heated in a big pan on med heat. Cook the leftover 2 garlic cloves for about thirty seconds or till fragrant. Put the leftover half-teaspoon of salt, cauliflower rice & 1/4 tsp pepper; stir-fry for three to five minutes or till softened. Whisk in the last 1/4 cup of coriander after removing it from the heat.

5. Distribute the cauliflower into Four bowls before serving. Add the black beans, avocado, sweet potato, & pico de gallo on top. Sprinkle the mojo sauce over each serving.

Nutritional Serving

344 Cal, Protein: 10.7g, Carb: 39g, Fat 18.1g

4.2 Butternut Squash Soup with Cheese Sandwiches (Apple Grilled)

Preparation Time: 15 mins

Cooking Time: 30 mins

Servings: 4

Ingredients

- Coconut oil/grapeseed oil, 2 tbsp

- Minced onion, 1 cup

- Chopped fresh ginger, 2 tbsp

- Ground cumin, 1 tsp

- Ground turmeric, 1 tsp

- Cayenne pepper, ¼ tsp

- Peeled & cubed butternut squash, 5 cups

- Light coconut milk, 1 can

- Chicken broth/no-chicken broth (reduced-sodium), 2 cups

- Finely sliced apple, 1

- Salt, ¾ tsp

- Lime juice, 1 tbsp

- Country bread(whole-wheat), 4 slices

- Cheddar cheese/shredded smoked gouda, 1 cup

- Ground pepper, pinch

Steps

1. In the saucepan, put one tbsp oil on med heat. Put ginger & onion. Cook for around 3 minutes while whisking often. Put turmeric, cayenne & cumin, then cook for 30 seconds while whisking. Put coconut milk, broth, squash, salt & apple slices half. Carry it to a simmer. Lower the heat & cook for around 20 minutes while sometimes whisking till the squash gets softer. Whisk in lime juice. Take it from heat.

2. Use the immersion blender to blend the soup in a pan.

3. Split half a cup of cheese among two bread slices. Put the leftover apple slices, bread & cheese on top. In the nonstick skillet, put the leftover 1 tbsp oil on med heat. Put the sandwiches & cook for around 2 minutes on each side or till their color changes to lightly brown on each side. Slice in half. Season the soup with the cayenne, ground pepper & stored coconut milk.

Nutritional Serving

419 Cal, Protein: 13.5g, Carb: 43.3g, Fat 23.1g

4.3 Honey Mustard Pork with Smashed White Beans and Spinach

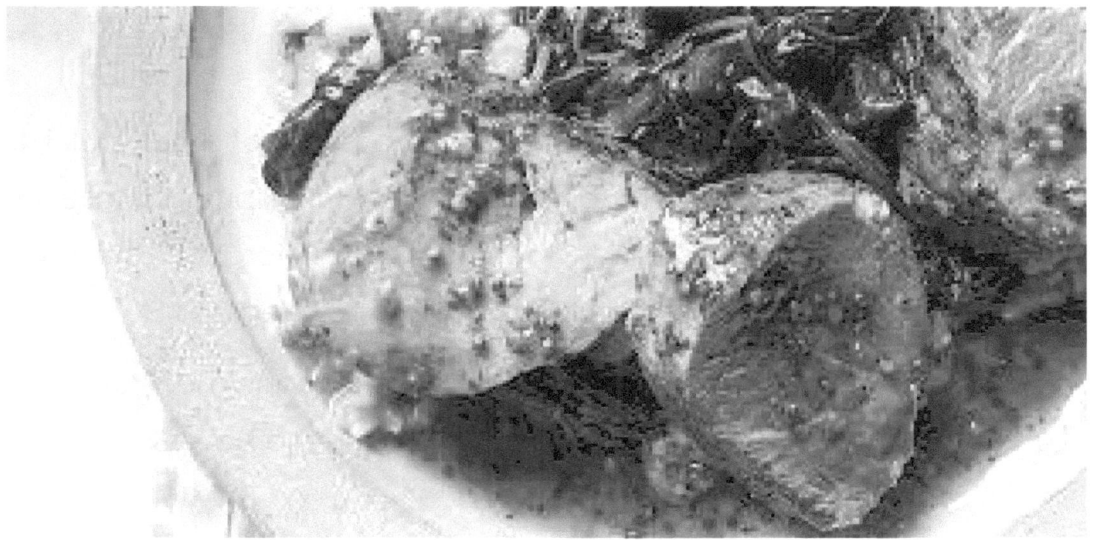

Preparation Time: 10 mins

Cooking Time: 20 mins

Servings: 4

Ingredients

- Trimmed pork tenderloin, 1¼ pounds

- Salt, ½ tsp

- Ground pepper, ½ tsp

- Olive oil(extra-virgin, 3 tbsp

- Minced mature spinach, 1 pound

- Chopped cloves garlic, 2

- Minced fresh sage, 1 ½ tsp

- Crushed red pepper, ¼ tsp

- Cannellini beans(reduced-sodium), 2 cans

- Chicken broth(reduced-sodium), ¾ cup

- Honey, 3 tbsp

- Mustard(whole-grain), 2 tbsp

Steps

1. Set the oven heat to 425 deg Fahrenheit.

2. Season the pork with pepper & 1/4 tsp salt. In the ovenproof skillet, put 1 tbsp oil on med heat. Put in the pork & cook for around 5 mins while flipping. Make sure that it's browned on all sides. Put the skillet in the oven. Roast for 12-15 minutes or till an immediate thermometer placed in the middle reads 145 degrees F.

3. In the big pot, put 1 tbsp oil on med heat in the meanwhile. Put 1/8 tsp salt & spinach, then cook for 3 minutes while whisking. Put it in the bowl & cover it to keep it hot.

4. In the pot, put the leftover 1 tbsp oil on med heat. Put sage, crushed red pepper & garlic, then cook for around thirty seconds. Put 1/2 cup broth, 1/8 tsp salt & beans. Use the potato masher to mash it till fully smooth. Lower the heat & cook for around 5 minutes while stirring frequently. Take it off from heat & Cover.

5. On the clean chopping board, move the pork & wait for five minutes. Put mustard, 1/4 cup broth & honey in the skillet. Carry to a simmer on med heat. Lower the heat & simmer for around 2 mins or till it's slightly thickened.

6. Cut the pork. Eat with mashed beans, sauce & spinach.

Nutritional Serving

499 Cal, Protein: 43g, Carb: 43.9g, Fat 16.6g

4.4 Broccoli and Scallion Ginger Beef

Preparation Time: 10 mins

Cooking Time: 20 mins

Servings: 4

Ingredients

- Reduced sodium soy sauce/tamari, 1/3 cup

- Reduced sodium chicken broth, ¼ cup

- Brown sugar, 2 tbsp

- Cornstarch, 2 tbsp

- Finely sliced sirloin steak, 1 pound

- Canola oil/peanut, 3 tbsp

- Broccoli florets, 6 cups

- Sliced scallions, ½ cup

- Thinly grated ginger, 1 tbsp

- Thinly grated garlic, 1 tsp

- Cooked brown rice, 2 cups

- Crushed red pepper, pinch

Steps

1. In the bowl, Stir together the broth, soy sauce/tamari, 1 tbsp cornstarch & brown sugar. Toss the steak with leftover one tbsp cornstarch.

2. In the cast-iron skillet, Put 2 tbsp oil on med heat. Put in the steak & cook for around 4 minutes while whisking once. Move it to the plate. Put in the broccoli & 1 tbsp oil, then cook for around 2 minutes while whisking occasionally. Whisk in ginger, garlic & scallions, then cook for around 30 seconds while stirring. Stir the tamari combination & add it to the beef. Put it in the skillet & cook for around 30 seconds till the sauce thickens.

3. Eat it on brown rice & season with crushed red pepper.

Nutritional Serving

441 Cal, Protein: 30g, Carb: 43.2g, Fat 16g

4.5 Carrots and Sheet-Pan Pork Chops (Maple-Mustard)

Preparation Time: 10 mins

Cooking Time: 30 mins

Servings: 4

Ingredients

- Olive oil(extra-virgin), 4 tbsp

- Whole-grain mustard, 1 tbsp

- Maple syrup, 1 tbsp

- 1/2 inch thick middle-sliced pork chops (bone-in) 5 ounces

- Rainbow carrots(sliced diagonally into 1/4-inch pieces) , 1 ½ pounds

- Thinly minced garlic, 2 tsp

- Peeled & coarsely minced fresh ginger, 1 tsp

- Ground turmeric, ½ tsp

- Kosher salt, ¾ tsp

- Ground pepper, ¾ tsp

- Minced flat-leaf parsley, ¼ cup

Steps

1. put your rack in the lowest oven's part, & preheat the rack to 430 degrees Fahrenheit.

2. In a bowl, stir maple syrup, 1 tbsp oil & mustard. On one side of the rimmed cookie sheet, put the chops of pork. With the oil combination, Brush the tops. Put the carrots on the other side & sprinkle with leftover three tbsp oil. Drizzle ginger, turmeric & garlic on carrots & toss to cover. Garnish everything with pepper & salt. Now Roast for around ten minutes.

3. Set the broiler heat to high. Around 4 minutes should be spent broiling till an immediate thermometer reads 145 degrees F when put into the thickest portion of the chop without contacting the bone. If necessary, simmer the carrots for an additional two to five minutes or until they are soft & glazed. Eat with parsley on top.

Nutritional Serving

376 Cal, Protein: 24.7g, Carb: 20.9g, Fat 21.1g

4.6 Golden Veggie Soup

Preparation Time: 30 mins

Cooking Time: 50 mins

Servings: 4

Ingredients

- Olive oil(extra-virgin), 2 tbsp

- Minced yellow onion, 1

- Peeled butternut squash (sliced into one-inch pieces), 6 cups

- Seeded & minced serrano pepper, 1

- Chopped fresh ginger, 1 tbsp

- Ground coriander, 1 tsp

- Ground cumin, 1 tsp

- Ground turmeric, ½ tsp

- Fennel seeds(toasted), ¾ tsp

- Cauliflower florets, 2 cups

- Vegetable broth(low-sodium), 4 cups

- Light coconut milk(well-shaken), 1 ¼ cups

- Lime juice, 1 ½ tsp

- Salt, ½ tsp

Steps

1. On medium heat, warm the oil in a big Dutch oven/heavy stockpot. Put the onion as well as the squash; cook for approximately 7 minutes while stirring often or till the onion gets translucent. Whisk often while cooking the ginger & serrano for approximately a minute till fragrant.

2. Add cilantro, cumin, turmeric, & 1/4 tsp of fennel seeds after lowering the heat. Cook for approximately a minute while stirring continuously till fragrant. Whisk in the broth & cauliflower. On med heat, bring to a simmer; then, lower the heat & simmer for around thirty mins while whisking sometimes.

3. Put the squash combination into a blender while working in two batches. Remove the centerpiece from the blender & tighten the lid to let steam out. Put a fresh towel on the hole. Blend for 1 min, or till smooth. Put the mixture back in the pot.

4. Add one cup of coconut milk to the soup. On med heat, carry to a simmer. Add salt and lime juice, then stir. Take off the heat.

5. In four dishes, distribute the soup. Add a pinch of fennel seeds and one tbsp coconut milk to the top of each.

Nutritional Serving

262 Cal, Protein: 5g, Carb: 39g, Fat 12g

4.7 Vegetables and Ginger-Tahini Salmon (Oven-Baked)

Preparation Time: 20 mins

Cooking Time: 30 mins

Servings: 4

Ingredients

- Olive oil, 2 tbsp

- Cremini mushrooms/white button (sliced into one-inch chunks), 1 pound

- Salt, ½ tsp

- Minced sweet potato, 12 oz

- Trimmed green beans, 1 pound

- Soy sauce(low-sodium), 2 tbsp

- Tahini, 1 tbsp + 2 tsp

- Honey, 1 tbsp + 1 tsp

- Thinly grated ginger, 1 ½ tsp

- Salmon(sliced into four portions), 1 ¼ pounds

- Rice vinegar, 2 tsp

- Minced fresh chives, 2 tbsp

Steps

1. Put a big-rimmed cookie sheet in an oven. One rack should be placed in the center of the oven, & the other should be placed approximately six inches away from the broiler. Set the temperature to 425 degrees Fahrenheit.

2. In a large bowl, mix the mushrooms, sweet potato, 1 tbsp of oil, & 1/4 tsp of salt. Toss to cover.

3. From the oven, take out the baking sheet. On the pan, evenly distribute the vegetable combination; roast for about twenty minutes, stirring occasionally.

4. Green beans should be mixed with the leftover 1 tbsp oil & 1/4 tsp salt in the meanwhile. In a bowl, mix the tahini, soy sauce, honey, & ginger.

5. Take the pan out of the oven. Put your green beans on the opposite side of the sweet potatoes & mushrooms. If needed, nestle the salmon on top of the veggies & put it in the center. On top of the salmon, scatter half of the tahini sauce. For a further eight to ten minutes, roast the salmon till it flakes. After turning the broiler to high, broil for approximately three minutes or until the salmon becomes glazed.

6. The leftover tahini sauce should be mixed with vinegar before being drizzled over the salmon & veggies. If preferred, top with chives before serving.

Nutritional Serving

555 Cal, Protein: 37.7g, Carb: 37.3g, Fat 29.9g

4.8 Spinach Salad of Apple Cranberry along with Goat Cheese

Preparation Time: 10 mins

Cooking Time: 15 mins

Servings: 8

Ingredients

- Apple cider vinegar, 3 tbsp

- Spicy brown mustard, 4 tsp

- Pure maple syrup, 4 tsp

- Chopped shallot, 1 tbsp

- Kosher salt, ½ tsp

- Black pepper, ½ tsp

- Olive oil(extra-virgin), 3 tbsp

- Baby spinach, 10 ounces

- Finely sliced pink lady apples, 2

- Dried cranberries(sweetened), ½ cup

- Minced toasted pecans, ½ cup

- Crumbled goat cheese(semi-soft), ½ ounces

Steps

1. In a small bowl, Stir together mustard, vinegar, shallot, syrup, pepper & salt; Gradually stir in olive oil till fully mixed.

2. In the bowl, Toss together the apples, spinach, half of the pecans, dried cranberries & dressing. Move it to the serving plate & drizzle it with goat cheese & with leftover pecans. Serve right away.

Nutritional Serving

214 Cal, Protein: 4g, Carb: 22g, Fat 13g

4.9 Vegan Pumpkin Soup

Preparation Time: 15 mins

Cooking Time: 30 mins

Servings: 4

Ingredients

- Olive oil(extra-virgin), 2 tbsp
- Minced yellow onion, 1 cup
- Minced celery, 1 cup
- Chopped garlic, 1 tbsp
- Ground turmeric, 1 tsp
- Ground cumin, 1 tsp
- Ground ginger, ½ tsp
- Ground pepper, ½ tsp
- Pumpkin puree(unseasoned), 1 can
- Vegetable broth(low-sodium), 3 cups
- Salt, ½ tsp
- Coarsely minced roasted cashews(unsalted), ¾ cup
- Minced scallions, ¼ cup
- Smoked paprika, ½ tsp

Steps

1. In the saucepan, put oil on med heat. Put celery & onion, then cook for around seven minutes while whisking sometimes. Put turmeric, garlic, ginger, pepper & cumin, then cook for one min while whisking constantly. Put broth, pumpkin, 1/2 cup of cashews & salt. Carry to a simmer on high heat. Lower the heat to maintain the simmer, then cover & simmer for around fifteen mins or till the veggies become soft.

2. Into the blender, put the soup. Remove the centerpiece from the blender and tighten the lid to let steam out. Put the clean cloth on the hole. Blend for around thirty seconds till smooth. Put the soup equally into four bowls & drizzle with paprika, scallions & with the leftover 1/4 cup of cashews.

Nutritional Serving

298 Cal, Protein: 6.6g, Carb: 28.9g, Fat 19.3g

4.10 Tofu Curry and Delicata Squash

Preparation Time: 15 mins

Cooking Time: 30 mins

Servings: 4

Ingredients

- Curry powder, 2 tbsp

- Salt, ½ tsp

- Ground pepper, ¼ tsp

- Firm water-packed tofu, 1 14-ounce package

- Canola oil, 4 tsp

- Halved & seeded delicata squash(sliced into one inch cubes), 1 pound

- Halved & sliced onion, 1

- Shredded fresh ginger, 2 tsp

- lite coconut milk, 1 14-ounce can

- Light brown sugar, 1 tsp

- Coarsely minced chard/ kale(tough stems trimmed), 8 cups

- Lime juice, 1 tbsp

Steps

1. In the bowl, mix salt, pepper & curry powder. Cut the tofu into one-inch cubes after patting it dry with the paper towel; in the bowl, toss the tofu with 1 tsp of a spice combination.

2. In the nonstick skillet, put 2 tsp oil on med heat. Put the tofu & cook while whisking every two mins, till browned; it will take around 6-8 mins in total. Move to the plate.

3. On med heat, put the leftover 2 tsp oil. Put onion, squash, leftover spice mixture & ginger; then cook for around 5 mins while whisking. Put in the brown sugar & coconut milk; carry to a simmer. Put half of the kale & cook for around one min while whisking. Mix in the remaining greens & cook for 1 minute while stirring. Put the tofu back in the skillet, cover it & cook for further five mins while whisking sometimes. Cook till the greens & squash becomes tender. Take the skillet off the heat & whisk in lime juice.

Nutritional Serving

316 Cal, Protein: 15.8g, Carb: 29.3g, Fat 18.2g

4.11 Ginger Beef Whisk-Fry along with Peppers

Preparation Time: 10 mins

Cooking Time: 25 mins

Servings: 4

Ingredients

- Trimmed lean flank steak, 12 ounces

- Cornstarch, 1 ½ tsp

- Soy sauce(low-sodium), 1 tbsp

- Dry sherry, 1 tsp + 1 tbsp

- Vegetable oil, 1 tsp + 1 tbsp

- Hoisin sauce, 4 tsp

- Ketchup, 4 tsp

- Sriracha/chili-garlic sauce, 1-3 tsp

- Peeled & smashed ginger, 3 slices

- Finley sliced yellow onion, 1

- Chopped green bell pepper, 1 cup

- Chopped red bell pepper, 1 cup

- Beef broth(unsalted), 2 tbsp

Steps

1. Slice the beef with grain into two-inch-thick strips. Slice every strip across the grain into the quartered inch-thick pieces. Mix the and cornstarch, beef, 1 tsp sherry & 1½ tsp soy sauce in the bowl; Whisk until there is no longer any cornstarch to be seen. Put 1 tsp oil & whisk till the beef is softly coated.

2. Mix ketchup, hoisin sauce, leftover 1½ tsp soy sauce, 1 tbsp sherry & chili-garlic sauce in the bowl. Put aside.

3. A 12-inch stainless steel pan or a 13.5-inch plain carbon steel wok should be heated on high heat till a drop of water evaporates within one to two seconds. Add the leftover 1 Tbsp. Of oil & stir. Put the ginger & stir-fry for approximately ten seconds, or till fragrant. Add the meat in an equal layer and press the ginger to the edges of the pan. Cook the meat for approximately a minute without stirring or till it starts to brown. Put the onion, then stir-fry for a further 1 minute. Onto a dish, put the beef & onion combination.

4. Put the broth in the pan along with the green & red peppers. With the lid on, cook for around a min on high heat or till the peppers become bright green & red, and nearly

all the fluid has been absorbed. Bring the beef, onion, as well as any remaining liquids back into the pan. Stir-fry the beef with the saved sauce for 1 minute or till the steak is just done, as well, as the peppers are crisp-tender.

Nutritional Serving

215 Cal, Protein: 20g, Carb: 11g, Fat 10g

4.12 Chicken Soup of Filipino Ginger Garlic (Tinola)

Preparation Time: 15 mins

Cooking Time: 30 mins

Servings: 4

Ingredients

- Avocado oil/canola oil, 3 tbsp

- Minced yellow onion, ½ cup

- Finely sliced fresh ginger, ¼ cup

- Minced cloves of garlic, 6

- Skinless & boneless chicken thighs(sliced into half inch pieces), 1 pound

- Chicken broth(reduced-sodium), 4 cups

- Peeled & cubed chayote/green papaya, 1 ½ cups

- Minced bok choy leaves/malunggay leaves, 2 cups

- Fish sauce, 1 tbsp

- Salt, ¼ tsp

- Ground black pepper, ¼ tsp

Steps

1. In the big pot, put oil on med heat. Put ginger, garlic & onion; then cook for around three minutes while whisking. Cook till the onion begins to become translucent. Put

broth & chicken; then cook for around five mins while whisking. Cook till the chicken is fully cooked. Put malunggay leaves, fish sauce, salt, pepper & papaya; continue to simmer for around five mins or till the veggies become soft & the flavors have combined.

Nutritional Serving

344 Cal, Protein: 27.4g, Carb: 14.2g, Fat 20.5g

4.13 Combined Greens with Sliced Apple and Lentils

Preparation Time: 5 mins

Cooking Time: 10 mins

Servings: 1

Ingredients

- Combined salad greens, 1 ½ cups

- Cooked lentils, ½ cup

- Cored & sliced apple, 1

- Grated feta cheese, 1 ½ tbsp

- Red-wine vinegar, 1 tbsp

- Olive oil(extra-virgin), 2 tsp

Steps

1. Put half of the apple slices, feta & lentils on top of the greens. Sprinkle with oil & vinegar. Eat with the leftover slices of apple on the side.

Nutritional Serving

347 Cal, Protein: 12.7g, Carb: 48.1g, Fat 13.2g

4.14 Beef Balti and Lamb

Preparation Time: 15 mins

Cooking Time: 30 mins

Servings: 4

Ingredients

- Water, 1 ½ cups

- Brown basmati rice, 1 cup

- Lean ground beef, 8 ounces

- Ground lamb, 8 ounces

- Minced yellow onions, 3 cups

- Minced garlic, 2 tbsp

- Ground turmeric, 1 tbsp

- Grated ginger, 2 tsp

- Ground coriander, 1 ½ tsp

- Ground cumin, 1 tsp

- Tomato paste, 3 tbsp

- Beef broth(unsalted), 3 cups

- Worcestershire sauce, 2 tbsp

- Salt, ¾ tsp

- Plain Greek yogurt(Reduced-fat), ¼ cup

- Minced fresh coriander, 3 tbsp

Steps

1. In the saucepan, mix water & rice; carry to a simmer on high heat. Lower the heat & cover it, then cook for around 40 minutes or till the water is absorbed,

2. Cook lamb & beef for around 6 mins in the big skillet on med heat. Put in the onions & cook for around seven mins while whisking occasionally.

3. Turn up the heat to high. Put turmeric, garlic, coriander, cumin & ginger; cook for around one minute while whisking. Whisk in the tomato paste & cook for 1 minute while stirring. Whisk in Worcestershire, salt & broth; carry to a simmer. Lower the heat & simmer for around 15 minutes while stirring sometimes.

4. Eat the Balti with the rice, garnished with coriander & some yogurt.

Nutritional Serving

531 Cal, Protein: 31.2g, Carb: 58g, Fat 19.5g

4.15 Apple Soup and Curried Parsnip

Preparation Time: 20 mins

Cooking Time: 45 mins

Servings: 4

Ingredients

- Olive oil(extra-virgin), 1 tbsp

- Cored, peeled & minced parsnips, 1 ½ pounds

- Thinly chopped onion, 1

- Thinly chopped cloves of garlic, 3

- Chicken broth(reduced-sodium), 4 cups

- Water, 1 cup

- Peeled & chopped russet potato, 1

- Peeled & minced granny smith apple, 1

- Mild curry powder, 1 ½ tsp

- Ground coriander, 1 ½ tsp

- Ground cumin, 1 tsp

- Ground ginger, ½ tsp

- Lemon juice, 4 tsp

- Salt, ½ tsp

- Ground pepper, ¼ tsp

- Plain yogurt(reduced-fat), ½ cup

Steps

1. In a large pot, put oil on med heat. Put in onion & parsnips, then cook for around 6 mins while whisking occasionally. Cook till the onion starts to brown. Put garlic & cook for 1 min while whisking occasionally. Put water, broth, apple, potato, curry powder, cumin, ginger & coriander; carry to a simmer. Cover it & lower the heat & simmer for around twenty mins or till the veggies become tender.

2. With the immersion blender, blend the soup in a pot till smooth. Put salt, pepper & lemon juice. Sprinkle the coriander on top & eat with dollops of yogurt swirled on top.

Nutritional Serving

303 Cal, Protein: 7.9g, Carb: 57.6g, Fat 5.8g

4.16 Stuffed Chicken Quinoa Salad

Preparation Time: 5 mins

Cooking Time: 5 mins

Servings: 1

Ingredients

- Grated cooked chicken breast, ¾ cup

- Cooked quinoa, ½ cup

- Roasted root veggies, 1 cup

- Vinaigrette, 1 to 2 tbsp

- Sliced avocado, ¼

- Crushed feta cheese, 1 tbsp

- Sunflower seeds, 1 tbsp

Steps

1. In the bowl, mix quinoa, roasted veggies & chicken; Sprinkle with vinaigrette. Garnish with feta, sunflower seeds & avocado.

Nutritional Serving

499 Cal, Protein: 23.2g, Carb: 40.7g, Fat 27.7g

4.17 Roasted Carrot Soup

Preparation Time: 20 mins

Cooking Time: 50 mins

Servings: 4

Ingredients

- Peeled carrots(Sliced into 2-3 inch chunks), 1 ½ pounds

- Peeled & quartered onion, 1

- Unpeeled cloves of garlic, 1

- Peeled & sliced fresh ginger, 1 piece

- Olive oil, 1 tbsp

- Almond milk(unsweetened), 2 cups

- Coarsely ground black pepper, 1 tsp

- Chicken broth(reduced-sodium), 1 cup

- Water, 1 cup

- Shredded carrot, 1 tsp

- Basil leave, 1

Steps

1. Set the oven temp to 400 deg Fahrenheit. Combine the onion, carrot pieces, ginger & garlic in the bowl. Sprinkle with the olive oil, then toss to cover. Place the veggies on a baking tray that is 15 by 10 by 1 inch. Bake for around one hour or till carrots become tender. Slightly Cool it.

2. Put garlic cloves in the blender after removing their skins. Put onion, ginger & roasted carrots, then cover it & process till the veggies are minced. Put broth, pepper & almond milk. Cover & blend/process till smooth.

3. Move to the saucepan. Whisk in water. Cook & whisk till fully heated. Season with basil leaves & shredded carrot, If needed.

Nutritional Serving

138 Cal, Protein: 3.1g, Carb: 21g, Fat 5.1g

4.18 Beef Stir Fry with Ginger and Baby Bok Choy

Preparation Time: 10 mins

Cooking Time: 15 mins

Servings: 4

Ingredients

- Trimmed beef flank steak, 12 ounces

- Chopped fresh ginger, 1 tbsp

- Soy sauce(low-sodium), 1 ½ tsp

- Dry sherry, 1 tsp + 1 tbsp

- Cornstarch, 1 tsp

- Toasted sesame oil, 1 tsp

- Oyster-flavored sauce, 2 tbsp

- Vegetable oil, 1 tbsp

- Trimmed baby bok choy(sliced into two-inch pieces), 1 pound

- Chicken broth(unsalted), 3 tbsp

Steps

1. Into two-inch-thick strips, slice the beef with a grain. Slice every strip across the grain into quartered inch-thick pieces. In the bowl, mix the ginger, beef, 1 tsp sherry, cornstarch & soy sauce; whisk till the cornstarch cannot be seen. Put in sesame oil & whisk till the beef is coated lightly.

2. In the bowl, mix the oyster-flavored sauce with the leftover 1 tbsp sherry. Put aside.

3. Over high heat, put the fourteen-inch carbon-steel wok(flat-bottomed) till the water drop evaporates within two seconds. Put in the vegetable oil. Put the beef in an equal layer & heat it for about one minute, occasionally stirring, till it starts to brown. Stir-fry for an additional one minute, often stirring, until the food is lightly browned while not fully done. Place on a platter.

4. Put broth & bok choy in the skillet. Cover it & cook for around two mins or till the bok choy greens become bright green & almost all of the water has been taken in. Put the beef back in the skillet, put the leftover sauce, & stir-fry for around one min or till the beef is fully cooked & the bok choy becomes tender and crispy.

Nutritional Serving

247 Cal, Protein: 25.5g, Carb: 6.3g, Fat 12.8g

4.19 Arugula Salad with Pears, Blue Cheese and Roasted Pork Tenderloin

Preparation Time: 15 mins

Cooking Time: 35 mins

Servings: 4

Ingredients

- Minced walnuts, 2 tbsp

- Balsamic vinegar, 3 tbsp

- Olive oil(extra-virgin), 2 tbsp

- Lemon juice, 2 tsp

- Honey, 1 tsp

- Dijon mustard, 1 tsp

- Thinly minced fresh rosemary, 2 tsp

- Chopped clove garlic, 1

- Salt, ½ tsp

- Ground pepper, ½ tsp

- Pork tenderloin, 1 pound

- Arugula, 8 cups

- Small red pears(cut into pieces), 4

- Grated blue cheese, ¼ cup

Steps

1. Set the oven temp to 400 deg Fahrenheit. With cooking spray, Coat the big-rimmed cookie sheet.

2. In the skillet, Cook the walnuts on med heat while whisking often. Cook till it gets golden & fragrant. Put aside.

3. In the bowl, stir oil, vinegar, honey, lemon juice, rosemary, mustard, garlic, & 1/4 tsp of each pepper & salt. On the prepared cookie sheet, put the pork. Brush with one tbsp dressing & drizzle with leftover 1/4 tsp each pepper & salt.

4. Roast the pork for 18 to 20 mins, till a thermometer reads 145 degrees F.

5. Put it on the chopping board & let it wait for five mins. Slice into 3/4 inch thick

6. Pieces.

7. In the large bowl, Put pears & arugula on the dressing & toss to cover. Put the salad between four plates. Garnish with the cheese, pork & leftover walnuts.

Nutritional Serving

352 Cal, Protein: 27g, Carb: 25.4g, Fat 15.9g

4.20 Broccoli and Ginger Roasted Salmon

Preparation Time: 10 mins

Cooking Time: 15 mins

Servings: 4

Ingredients

- Dark sesame oil (toasted), 1 ½ tbsp

- Tamari(low-sodium), 1 ½ tbsp

- Rice vinegar, 1 ½ tbsp

- Shredded fresh ginger, 1 tbsp

- Broccoli florets with two-inch stalks, 8 cups

- Salt, ¼ tsp

- Molasses, 1 tbsp

- Wild salmon(sliced into four portions), 1 ¼ pounds

- Sesame seeds(toasted), 2 tsp

Steps

1. Set the oven temp to 425 deg Fahrenheit. With cooking spray, coat the rimmed cookie sheet.

2. In the bowl, stir tamari, oil, ginger, 1/8 tsp salt & vinegar. Put in the broccoli & toss to cover. Using tongs/slotted spoon, move to the preheated pan, reserving as much marinade as possible in the bowl. Stir the leftover marinade with molasses.

3. For five minutes, roast the broccoli. Put it to pan's one side of the & put salmon on the different side. Garnish the salmon with leftover 1/8 tsp salt & coat with a molasses

glaze. For a further seven to ten minutes, roast the salmon till it is just cooked completely. Drizzle sesame seeds on top.

Nutritional Serving

323 Cal, Protein: 33.6g, Carb: 16.8g, Fat 13.2g

4.21 Soup of Vegan Carrot Ginger

Preparation Time: 20 mins

Cooking Time: 40 mins

Servings: 6

Ingredients

- Olive oil(extra-virgin), ¼ cup

- Peeled & minced carrots, 2 pounds

- Finely sliced sweet onion, 2 cups

- Finely sliced garlic, 1 tbsp

- Chopped fresh ginger, 1 tbsp

- Cumin seeds, 2 tsp

- Coriander seeds, 2 tsp

- Vegetable broth/carrot juice, 4 cups

- Harissa, 2 tbsp

- Salt, ¼ tsp

- Sliced toasted almonds, ¼ cup

- Minced fresh coriander, 2 tbsp

- Grated lime zest, 1 tsp

- Lime juice, 1 tsp

Steps

1. In the big heavy pot, put 1 tbsp oil on med heat. Put the onion & carrots, then cover it & cook for around 4 minutes till softened. Put ginger, garlic, coriander & cumin. Cook for around 1 minute while uncovered & constantly whisking till fragrant. Whisk in harissa, salt & carrot juice; carry to a simmer on med heat. Lower the heat & simmer for around 20 minutes while whisking occasionally.

2. In the bowl, stir cilantro, lime zest & almonds together in the meanwhile.

3. In a blender, put the soup. Remove the centerpiece, attach the blender's lid, and close the hole with the dry cloth. Run the blender for around one min, after which add 2 tbsp of oil while it is running. (an immersion blender can also blend the soup in a pot for approximately one min.) Add lime juice & stir.

4. Pour the soup into eight bowls & top with the almond combination. Sprinkle the leftover 1 tbsp oil & serve right away

Nutritional Serving

245 Cal, Protein: 5g, Carb: 31g, Fat 12g

4.22 Sesame Chicken(Sheet-Pan) and Broccoli along with Scallion Ginger Sauce

Preparation Time: 20 mins

Cooking Time: 40 mins

Servings: 4

Ingredients

- Broccoli florets with two-inch stalks, 8 cups

- Sesame oil, 2 tbsp

- Salt, 1 tsp

- Ground pepper, ½ tsp

- Trimmed & bone-in chicken thighs, 2 pounds

- Avocado oil, 2 tbsp

- Chopped scallion, 3 tbsp

- Chopped fresh ginger, 2 tsp

- Rice vinegar, 1 tsp

- Sesame seeds(toasted), 2 tsp

Steps

1. In the oven, put the big-rimmed cookie sheet. Set the oven heat to 425 deg f.

2. In a large bowl, mix 1 tbsp sesame oil, broccoli, 1/4 tsp each pepper & salt. In a different bowl, toss the chicken with leftover 1 tbsp sesame oil & 1/4 tsp each pepper & salt.

3. On one side of the hot pan, put the chicken in one layer while the skin side down. Now roast for fifteen min. Put the broccoli onto the pan's other side after flipping the chicken over. Cook for another twenty to twenty-five minutes, flipping the broccoli midway thru or till the chicken is fully cooked & the broccoli gets soft.

4. In the meanwhile, bring a small pan on med heat. Put the leftover 1/2 tsp salt, vinegar, scallion, ginger, and avocado oil, & simmer for 15 seconds while stirring. Turn off the heat.

5. Eat the broccoli & chicken sprinkled with the sesame seeds & scallion-ginger sauce.

Nutritional Serving

422 Cal, Protein: 36.5g, Carb: 8.2g, Fat 27.5g

4.23 Pumpkin Curry Soup

Preparation Time: 25 mins

Cooking Time: 35 mins

Servings: 6

Ingredients

- Olive oil(extra-virgin), 2 tbsp

- Minced sweet onion, 2 cups

- Minced celery, ¾ cup

- Minced carrot, ¾ cup

- Smashed cloves of garlic, 4

- Peeled & finely sliced ginger, 1 piece

- Seeded & chopped jalapeño pepper, 1

- Madras curry powder, 1 tbsp

- Ground allspice, 1 tsp

- Bay leaves, 2

- Pumpkin puree(unseasoned), 2 cans

- Vegetable broth(low-sodium), 4 cups

- Salt, ¾ tsp

- Well-shaken coconut milk, 1 can

- Fresh lime juice, 2 tbsp

- Minced dry-roasted peanuts(unsalted), 6 tbsp

Steps

1. In the big heavy pot, put oil on med heat. Put celery, carrot & onion, then cook for around 5 minutes while whisking often. Put ginger, garlic, curry powder, jalapeño, bay leaves & allspice, then cook for around 1 min while whisking constantly.

2. In the pot, put broth, salt & pumpkin; carry it to a simmer on med heat. Lower the heat, then cover it & simmer till the veggies become tender. It will take around 25 mins.

3. Take away the bay leaves. Into the blender, pour the soup. Put 6 tbsp of coconut milk in a small dish & set it aside for serving. Fill the blender with the leftover coconut milk. Take the centerpiece from the blender & tighten the lid to let steam out. Put a dry cloth over the hole. For approximately 30 seconds, blend till smooth. Put the soup

back in the pot. (Alternatively, mix the soup & coconut milk in the pot at high speed for 2 to 3 minutes, or till smooth.) Bring back to a boil over med heat. Take the heat off and add lime juice.

4. Pour the soup equally into 6 dishes, top with the coconut milk set aside, and garnish with peanuts. If wanted, add more jalapenos as a garnish.

Nutritional Serving

327 Cal, Protein: 6.5g, Carb: 27.8g, Fat 23.8g

4.24 Kale Frittata and Cauliflower

Preparation Time: 15 mins

Cooking Time: 30 mins

Servings: 4

Ingredients

- Olive oil(extra-virgin), 2 tbsp

- Sliced onion, 1

- Cauliflower florets, 2 cups

- Water, ¼ cup

- Minced kale, 5 cups

- Minced cloves of garlic, 3

- Chopped fresh thyme, 1 tsp

- Salt, ½ tsp

- Ground pepper, ½ tsp

- Eggs, 8

- Smoked paprika, ½ tsp

- Crumbled manchego cheese/ shredded goat cheese, ½ cup

Steps

1. Put the rack in the oven's upper third; Set the broiler temp to high.

2. In the big cast-iron skillet, put 1 tbsp oil on med heat. Put onion & cook for around four mins while whisking occasionally. Put water & cauliflower. Cover & cook for around 6 minutes or till it gets tender. Put garlic, kale, thyme & ¼ tsp each pepper & salt, then cook for around three mins while often whisking, till the kale is wilted.

3. In the bowl, stir paprika, eggs & the leftover ¼ tsp pepper & salt. Put the veggies into the mixture of an egg; whisk to combine. Clean the pan & then put the leftover 1 tbsp oil & heat on med heat. Put in the mixture of egg & drizzle with cheese. Then Cover & cook for around five mins or till the sides are ready & the bottom gets brown.

4. On to the oven, put the pan & broil for around three mins or till the frittata top is cooked.

Nutritional Serving

293 Cal, Protein: 17.9g, Carb: 7.9g, Fat 21.1g

Chapter 5: Snack Recipes

5.1 Chocolate-Peanut Butter Energy Bars

Preparation Time: 25 mins

Cooking Time: 1 hr

Servings: 16

Ingredients

- Medjool dates (chopped), ¾ cup

- Peanut butter (smooth natural), 1 cup

- Rolled oats, ½ cup

- salt, ¼ tsp

- Dry-roasted peanuts (chopped & unsalted), ½ cup

- Chocolate chips (bittersweet), ¾ cup

Steps

1. In a medium dish, cover dates with boiling water and let them soak for ten minutes. Reserve the soaking water and drain.

2. In the meantime, line a baking dish that is 8 inches square with parchment paper, allowing excess to hang over the two edges. Spray some cooking spray on the parchment paper lightly.

3. Mix the soaked dates, nut butters, oats, and salt in a food processor. Process until the mixture is very finely chopped & beginning to clump together. Add a bit of the saved soaking water, 1 tbsp at a time, if the mixture appears dry. Add peanuts to the small bowl after transfer. In the prepared pan, distribute the ingredients firmly and uniformly.

4. In a microwave-safe dish, add the chocolate chips, & microwave on medium for two to three minutes or until completely melted. Over the oat mixture, evenly distribute the chocolate. For about an hour, refrigerate until chilled. Lift the hanging parchment to remove from the pan. Into 16 squares, cut.

Nutritional Serving

203 Cal, Protein: 5.4g, Carb: 17.4g, Fat 12.7g

5.2 Avocado Hummus

Preparation Time: 5 mins

Cooking Time: 10 mins

Servings: 10

Ingredients

- Chickpeas (no-salt-added), 1 (15-ounce) can

- ripe avocado (halved & pitted), 1

- fresh cilantro leaves, 1 cup

- tahini, ¼ cup

- olive oil (extra-virgin), ¼ cup

- lemon juice, ¼ cup

- garlic, 1 clove

- ground cumin, 1 tsp

- salt, ½ tsp

Steps

1. Chickpeas should be drained, with tbsp of the liquid saved. Add the chickpeas & the liquid you set aside to a food processor. Avocado, cilantro, oil, tahini, lime juice, garlic, cumin, and salt should all be added until very smooth and pure. Serve with crudités, pita chips, or vegetable chips.

Nutritional Serving

156 Cal, Protein: 3.3g, Carb: 9.5g, Fat 12.4g

5.3 Strawberry-Chocolate Greek Yogurt Bark

Preparation Time: 40 mins

Cooking Time: 2 hrs 30 mins

Servings: 32

Ingredients

- Plain Greek yogurt (whole milk), 3 cups

- Honey pure or maple syrup, ¼ cup

- Vanilla extract, 1 tsp

- Strawberries (sliced), 1 ½ cups

- Chocolate chips, ¼ cup

Steps

1. Use parchment paper to line a baking sheet with a rim.

2. In a medium bowl, combine yogurt, maple syrup (or honey), and vanilla. Spread into a 10- by 15-inch rectangle on the baking sheet that has been prepared. Add the strawberries and chocolate chips to the surface.

3. Freeze for at least 3 hours or until extremely stiff. Cut or split into 32 pieces to serve.

Nutritional Serving

34 Cal, Protein: 2g, Carb: 4g, Fat 1.3g

5.4 Peanut Butter Energy Balls

Preparation Time: 5 mins

Cooking Time: 15 mins

Servings: 17

Ingredients

- Rolled oats, 2 cups

- Nut butter or natural peanut butter, 1 cup

- Honey, ½ cup

- Mini chocolate chips, ¼ cup

- Shredded coconut (unsweetened), ¼ cup

Steps

1. In a medium bowl, combine the oats, honey, chocolate chips, peanut butter, and coconut. Stir well. Roll the dough into 1-tablespoon-sized balls.

Nutritional Serving

174 Cal, Protein: 4.4g, Carb: 18.2g, Fat 9.2g

5.5 Lemon-Blueberry Bars

Preparation Time: 30 mins

Cooking Time: 2 hrs 10 mins

Servings: 9

Ingredients

- Graham cracker crumbs, 1 ¼ cups

- Salted butter (melted), 4 tbsp

- Granulated sugar, 1 tbsp

- Lemon zest, 1

- Condensed milk (sweetened), 1 (14-ounce) can

- Lemon juice, ½ cup

- Large egg, 1

- Fresh blueberries, 1 cup

Steps

1. Set the oven to 350°F. Spray cooking spray in an 8-inch square baking pan.

2. In a medium bowl, combine the graham crumbs, butter, sugar, and half of the lemon zest. In the prepared pan, evenly and firmly press the ingredients. About 10 minutes of baking time is required to gently brown the edges. At least 10 mins should pass while the pan is cooling on a wire rack.

3. Condensed milk, lime juice, egg, and the leftover lemon zest are completely combined in a medium bowl during this time. Add blueberries and stir.

4. Over the cooked crust, evenly distribute the filling. Bake for 16 to 18 minutes or until set. Allow to cool for an hour at room temperature. For one additional hour at least, cover and chill.

Nutritional Serving

273 Cal, Protein: 5g, Carb: 40g, Fat 11g

5.6 Garlic Hummus

Preparation Time: 5 mins

Cooking Time: 10 mins

Servings: 8

Ingredients

- No-salt chickpeas, 1 (15-ounce) can

- Tahini, ¼ cup

- Olive oil (extra-virgin), ¼ cup

- Lemon juice, ¼ cup

- Garlic, 1 clove

- Ground cumin, 1 tsp

- Chili powder, ½ tsp

- Salt, ½ tsp

Steps

1. Chickpeas should be drained, saving 1/4 cup of a liquid. Add the chickpeas & the liquid you set aside to a stick blender. Add the salt, tahini, garlic, lemon juice, oil, cumin, & chili powder. Puree for 2 to 3 minutes, or until extremely smooth.

Nutritional Serving

155 Cal, Protein: 3.7g, Carb: 9.7g, Fat 11.9g

5.7 Almost Chipotle's Guacamole

Preparation Time: 10 mins

Cooking Time: 10 mins

Servings: 8

Ingredients

- Ripe avocados (medium), 3

- Jalapeño pepper (finely chopped), 1 medium

- Red or white onion (finely chopped), ¼ cup

- Fresh cilantro (chopped), ¼ cup

- Lime juice, 2 tbsp

- Garlic (grated), 1 clove

- Salt, ½ tsp

Steps

1. With a fork, mash the avocados inside a medium basin. Stir in the jalapenos, onions, cilantro, lime juice, garlic, and salt after adding them.

Nutritional Serving

125 Cal, Protein: 1.6g, Carb: 7.5g, Fat 11.1g

5.8 Raspberry-Lemon Greek Frozen Yogurt Bark

Preparation Time: 15 mins

Cooking Time: 3 hrs

Servings: 16

Ingredients

- Plain Greek yogurt (whole milk), 3 cups

- Honey, ¼ cup

- Lemon Zest, 1

- Lemon juice, 2 tbsp

- Vanilla extract, 1 tsp

- Raspberries (halved lengthwise), 6 ounces

Steps

1. Use parchment paper to line a big baking sheet with a rim.

2. In a medium bowl, combine yogurt, honey, lemon juice, and vanilla. Spread into a 10- by 15-inch rectangle on the baking sheet that has been prepared. Add some lemon zest and raspberries on the top.

3. Freeze for at least 3 hours or until extremely stiff. Cut or split into 32 pieces to serve.

Nutritional Serving

69 Cal, Protein: 5g, Carb: 8g, Fat 3g

5.9 Roasted Buffalo Chickpeas

Preparation Time: 10 mins

Cooking Time: 30 mins

Servings: 4

Ingredients

- white vinegar, 1 tbsp

- cayenne pepper, ½ tsp

- salt, ¼ tsp

- chickpeas (no-salt-added), 15 ounces

Steps

1. The oven rack should be in upper third; heat to 400 ° F.

2. Salt, cayenne, and vinegar are combined in a large basin. Chickpeas should be dried very completely before being mixed with the vinegar mixture. Spread on a baking sheet with a rim. For 30 to 35 minutes, roast the chickpeas, tossing twice, until they are crisp and golden. The chickpeas will become crisp as they cool; leave to cool for 30 minutes on the pan.

Nutritional Serving

109 Cal, Protein: 5.8g, Carb: 17.6g, Fat 0.9g

5.10 Chickpea Snack Salad

Preparation Time: 5 mins

Cooking Time: 5 mins

Servings: 1

Ingredients

- Canned chickpeas (rinsed), ½ cup

- Grape tomatoes halved, ¼ cup

- Pitted olives (sliced), 2

- Red-wine vinaigrette, 1 tbsp

Steps

1. In a bowl, mix the chickpeas, tomatoes, and olives. Add vinaigrette & toss to coat after drizzle.

Nutritional Serving

202 Cal, Protein: 6g, Carb: 20g, Fat 11g

5.11 Mango-Date Energy Bites

Preparation Time: 5 mins

Cooking Time: 10 mins

Servings: 20

Ingredients

- Pitted whole dates, 2 cups

- Raw cashews, 1 cup

- Dried fruit or dried mango, 1 cup

- Salt, ¼ tsp

Steps

1. Mango (or other fruit), dates, cashews, and salt should all be coarsely minced in a food processor. Utilizing two teaspoons each ball, form into around 20 balls.

Nutritional Serving

73 Cal, Protein: 1.1g, Carb: 11g, Fat 3.3g

5.12 Date Energy Bites

Preparation Time: 5 mins

Cooking Time: 10 mins

Servings: 20

Ingredients

- Pitted whole dates, 2 cups

- Raw cashews, 1 cup

- Dried fruit or dried mango, 1 cup

- Salt, ¼ tsp

Steps

1. Mango (or other fruit), dates, cashews, and salt should all be coarsely minced in a food processor. Utilizing two teaspoons each ball, form into around 20 balls.

Nutritional Serving

73 Cal, Protein: 1.1g, Carb: 11g, Fat 3.3g

5.13 Vegan Chocolate-Dipped Frozen Banana Bites

Preparation Time: 30 mins

Cooking Time: 2 hrs

Servings: 24

Ingredients

- Bananas, 3 large

- Natural peanut butter, ¼ cup

- Vegan chocolate chips, ¾ cup

Steps

1. Each peeled banana should be split lengthwise. Spread peanut butter on each half. To make banana "sandwiches," combine the banana halves. From each banana "sandwich," cut 8 rounds. Place the frozen banana pieces on a baking sheet/tray that has been lined with parchment paper/wax paper & freeze for at least two hours or overnight.

2. In a microwave-safe dish, add the chocolate chips. Microwave on High for 1 to 1 1/2 minutes, stirring after each 15-second interval until completely melted. Each banana bite is coated with chocolate on one side. Let the chocolate stand until it has hardened. If not serving right away, put the food back in the freezer.

Nutritional Serving

58 Cal, Protein: 1g, Carb: 7.7g, Fat 3g

5.14 Peanut Butter-Oat Energy Balls

Preparation Time: 15 mins

Cooking Time: 20 mins

Servings: 12

Ingredients

- Medjool dates (chopped), ¾ cup

- rolled oats, ½ cup

- natural peanut butter, ¼ cup

- Chia seeds

Steps

1. Dates should be soaked for five to ten minutes in a small dish of boiling water. Drain.

2. Process the soaking dates, oats, and peanut butter until very finely ground in a food processor. Form into Twelve balls (a scant tbsp each). If desired, add chia seeds as a garnish. Place in the fridge for at least fifteen min & as long as a week.

Nutritional Serving

73 Cal, Protein: 1.8g, Carb: 10.1g, Fat 3g

5.15 Homemade Oven-Dried Strawberries

Preparation Time: 55 mins

Cooking Time: 3 hrs 30 mins

Servings: 3

Ingredients

- fresh strawberries (hulled & sliced), 1 pound (1/4 to 3/8 inch)

Steps

1. Set the oven to 200 °F. Use a silicone cooking mat to line a baking sheet with a rim. Place the strawberries cut side down on the baking sheet that has been prepared. Bake for about 4 hours, turning the strawberries once during that time.

2. Remove from oven & let baking sheet to cool fully, about 20 minutes.

Nutritional Serving

46 Cal, Protein: 1g, Carb: 11g, Fat 5g

5.16 Peanut Butter-S'mores Greek Yogurt Bark

Preparation Time: 30 mins

Cooking Time: 2 hrs 45 mins

Servings: 16

Ingredients

- Plain Greek yogurt (whole milk), 3 cups

- Honey, 2 tbsp

- Natural peanut butter, 1 tbsp

- Mini chocolate chips (semisweet), 2 tbsp

- Mini marshmallows, 2 tbsp

- Graham cracker crumbs, 3 tbsp

Steps

1. Using parchment paper or even a silicone baking mat, line a baking sheet with a rim. In a medium bowl, combine yogurt, honey, and peanut butter. Stir to thoroughly

combine. Just on prepared baking sheet, evenly distribute the ingredients. Sprinkle marshmallows, chocolate chips, & graham cracker crumbs on top.

2. Frozen for at least three hours, until solid. Cut or split into 32 pieces to serve.

Nutritional Serving

79 Cal, Protein: 5g, Carb: 8g, Fat 4g

5.17 Air-Fryer Crispy Chickpeas

Preparation Time: 10 mins

Cooking Time: 15 mins

Servings: 4

Ingredients

- Unsalted chickpeas (rinsed & drained), 15 ounce

- Toasted sesame oil, 1 ½ tbsp

- Smoked paprika, ¼ tsp

- Crushed red pepper, ¼ tsp

- Salt, ⅛ tsp

- Cooking spray

- Lime wedges, 2

Steps

1. On multiple layers of paper towels, spread the chickpeas. Roll the chickpeas beneath the towels to dry them on all sides, then add additional paper towels on top and pat until extremely dry.

2. In a medium bowl, mix the oil and chickpeas. Salt, crushed red pepper, and paprika should be added. Pour into a cooking spray-coated air fryer basket. Cook for 12 to 14 minutes at 400 degrees F, shaking the basket regularly until very nicely browned. Serve the chickpeas with lime wedges on top.

Nutritional Serving

132 Cal, Protein: 4.7g, Carb: 14.1g, Fat 5.8g

5.18 Beet Jerky

Preparation Time: 45 mins

Cooking Time: 4 hrs

Servings: 12

Ingredients

- Beets (scrubbed & trimmed), 1/2 pounds

- Vegan Worcestershire sauce, ¼ cup

- Reduced-sodium tamari, ¼ cup

- Pure maple syrup, 1 tsp

- Ground pepper, 1 tsp

- Onion powder, ½ tsp

- Garlic powder, ½ tsp

Steps

1. Using a mandolin, slice beets into 1/8-inch pieces.

2. In a big bowl, add Worcestershire, pepper, maple syrup, tamari, onion powder, & garlic powder. Beets should be added and coated. For at least two hours & up to two days, cover and chill the food.

3. Set the middle & lower oven rack positions, and heat the oven to 200 ° F. Two big baking sheets should be lined with parchment paper.

4. Eliminate the beets. Place on the preheated baking sheets in a single layer. (They can touch at the edges, but they shouldn't overlap.)

5. Bake for 2 1/2 to 2 3/4 hours, turning the pans top to bottom midway through, or till there is little to no liquid on the parchment paper & the beets are completely dry but still malleable.

Nutritional Serving

28 Cal, Protein: 1g, Carb: 6g, Fat 0.1g

5.19 Rice Cake Snackwich

Preparation Time: 5 mins

Cooking Time: 10 mins

Servings: 1

Ingredients

- Almond butter, 1 tbsp

- Brown rice cakes, 2

- Flaxseed, ½ tsp

- Pinch of ground cinnamon

- Apple (sliced), ½

Steps

1. On 1 rice cake, spread almond butter. Add cinnamon and flaxseed to the topping. Add other rice cake on top, then the apple.

Nutritional Serving

225 Cal, Protein: 5g, Carb: 31g, Fat 10g

5.20 Roasted Beet Hummus

Preparation Time: 10 mins

Cooking Time: 10 mins

Servings: 10

Ingredients

- No-salt-added chickpeas (rinsed), 1 (15-ounce) can

- Roasted beets (chopped), 8 ounces

- Tahini, ¼ cup

- Olive oil (extra-virgin), ¼ cup

- Lemon juice, ¼ cup

- Garlic, 1 clove

- Ground cumin, 1 tsp

- Salt, ½ tsp

Steps

1. In a food processor, mix chickpeas, beets, tahini, oil, lime juice, garlic, cumin, and salt. Puree for two to three minutes, or till extremely smooth. Serve with crudités, pita chips, or vegetable chips.

Nutritional Serving

133 Cal, Protein: 3.3g, Carb: 9.9g, Fat 9.5g

5.21 Raspberry-Pistachio Greek Yogurt Bark

Preparation Time: 40 mins

Cooking Time: 2 hrs 30 mins

Servings: 32

Ingredients

- Plain Greek yogurt (whole milk), 3 cups

- Pure honey or maple syrup, 2 tbsp

- Vanilla extract, 1 tsp

- Raspberry jam (no sugar added), 2 tbsp

- Pistachios (chopped), ¼ cup

Steps

1. Use parchment paper to line a baking sheet with a rim.

2. In a medium bowl, mix yogurt, maple syrup (or honey), and vanilla. Spread into a 10-by 15-inch rectangle on the baking sheet that has been prepared. Spread the jam liberally and twirl it with a knife. Add some pistachios on top.

3. Freeze for at least 3 hours, or until extremely stiff. Cut or split into 32 pieces to serve.

Nutritional Serving

31 Cal, Protein: 2.1g, Carb: 2.9g, Fat 1.3g

5.22 Peanut Butter-Date Energy Balls

Preparation Time: 10 mins

Cooking Time: 20 mins

Servings: 32

Ingredients

- Pitted dates (coarsely chopped), 2 ¼ cups

- Brown rice cereal or amaranth (puffed), ¾ cup

- Peanut butter, ¾ cup

- Ground flaxseed, 3 tbsp

- Pinch of salt

Steps

1. In a food processor, combine the cereal, dates, peanut butter, flaxseed, and salt when the mixture is crumbled but can be squeezed into a cohesive ball. Process for 10 to 20 pulses to finely chop the ingredients. After that, process for approximately a min, scraping the sides as needed.

2. Squeeze about 1 tbsp of the mixture firmly between your palms, then roll into a ball with damp hands (to stop the mixture from clinging to them). Place in a box for storage. The leftover mixture should be used again.

Nutritional Serving

75 Cal, Protein: 2g, Carb: 10.4g, Fat 3.4g

5.23 Salted Coconut-Caramel Energy Balls

Preparation Time: 15 mins

Cooking Time: 20 mins

Servings: 36

Ingredients

- Pitted dates, 4 dozen (about 3 cups)

- Sunflower seed butter (creamy), ¾ cup

- Warm water, 6 tbsp

- Kosher salt, 1 ½ tsp

- Vanilla extract, 1 ¼ tsp

- Rolled oats, 2 cups

- Toasted pecans (coarsely chopped), 6 tbsp

- Shredded coconut (unsweetened), ½ cup

Steps

1. In a blender, combine dates, sunflower butter, water, salt, and vanilla. Mix until nearly smooth with just few tiny particles of texture to a medium bowl, and transfer. Stir in the pecans and oats.

2. Put the coconut in a little basin. Make a ball out of a spoonful of the date mixture. (To avoid sticking, dampen your hands.) To coat, roll the ball inside the coconut. The leftover mixture should be used again.

Nutritional Serving

65 Cal, Protein: 1.8g, Carb: 5g, Fat 4.5g

Chapter 6: Salad, Dressing & Appetizer Recipes

6.1 Grilled Tomatoes

Preparation Time: 10 mins

Cooking Time: 30 mins

Servings: 5

Ingredients

Tahini-Caesar dressing

- Anchovy fillets (drained), 3 to 4 oil-packed

- Parmesan (finely grated), 1/4 cups

- Tahini, 1/4 cup

- Water, 3 tbsp

- Fresh lemon juice, 2 tbsp

- Freshly ground black pepper, 1/2 tsp

- Kosher salt

Tomatoes

- Beefsteak or heirloom tomatoes (large), 5 medium

- Olive oil (extra-virgin), 1 1/2 tbsp

- Oregano, 1 tbsp

- Kosher salt

- Black pepper (freshly ground)

- Parsley (chopped) & parmesan (shaved) for garnish

Steps

Tahini-Caesar Dressing

1. Anchovies, water, tahini, parmesan, lime juice, & black pepper should all be blended together until smooth. To get the required consistency, add 1 tsp of water at a time if the dressing is too thick.

2. Add salt to taste and transfer dressing to a small dish or airtight container. Up until usage, keep chilled.

3. Dressing can be prepared five days in advance. Remain cold.

Tomatoes

1. Take the stem and top core off of each tomato. Tomatoes should be cut in half horizontally & placed in a big basin.

2. Oil should be drizzled over the tomatoes before oregano, salt, and black pepper are added. Allow tomatoes to rest for 10 minutes after coating them. This will cause some liquid to leak out, allowing tomatoes to absorb flavor.

3. Grill at a medium-high temperature (between 400° & 450°). Grill tomato cut side down for eight to ten minutes, or until browned and starting to soften. After flipping, grill the tomatoes for a further five to seven minutes, or until they are soft but not mushy.

4. Place the tomatoes on a plate. Add parsley, Parmesan, and tahini-Caesar dressing as garnishes.

Nutritional Serving

40 Cal, Protein: 16g, Carb: 15g, Fat 1.2g

6.2 Chicken & Wild Rice Soup

Preparation Time: 20 mins

Cooking Time: 1 hr

Servings: 5

Ingredients

- Chicken thighs (bone in skin on), 1 lb. (about 3-4)

- Kosher salt

- Black pepper (freshly ground)

- Olive oil (extra-virgin), 1 tbsp.

- Red onion (chopped), 1 medium

- Shiitake mushrooms (chopped), 4 oz.

- Stalks celery (chopped), 2

- Garlic (chopped), 3 cloves

- Water, 6 cups

- Bay leaves (dried), 2

- Wild rice (rinsed), 1 cup

- Carrots, 2 medium (cut into ½" rounds)

- peeled russet potato, 1 (cut into ½" cubes)

- Curly torn kale (packed), 3 cups

- Fresh dill (chopped)

- Lemon wedges

Steps

1. The thighs' skins should be taken off (and set aside). Thoroughly salt and pepper the thighs, then put them aside.

2. Lay the skins flat in a big saucepan with the oil. Cook for about 10 min over medium heat, or till the skins are brown and crispy. Skins should be transferred with a slotted spoon to a dish covered with paper towels and salt. Let cool, then cut into irregular pieces with a knife.

3. To the saucepan, add red onions. After adding salt, sauté the onions for about 8 minutes, or until the edges start to brown.

4. Garlic, celery, and mushrooms should be added after a little salting. About 5 more minutes of cooking, stirring constantly will result in slightly softened mushrooms and celery.

5. Add the bay leaves, 1 tsp salt, and 6 cups of water, up to a boil. Simmer the mixture while adding the wild rice. Cook the saucepan for 20 minutes with the lid on.

6. To the saucepan, add the chicken thighs, carrots, and potatoes. Reduce to a simmer, cover, & cook for an additional 15 to 20 minutes, or until the rice is cooked through.

7. Take the saucepan off the heat. Transfer thighs to a chopping board using tongs. Add the kale to the broth and stir for 1 minute.

8. Chicken may be shredded into bite-sized pieces using two forks. Return meat to a broth after discarding the bones.

9. If extra salt and pepper are required, taste the soup & adjust the seasoning. Pour into bowls and garnish with lemon juice, dill, and crispy chicken skin.

Nutritional Serving

83 Cal, Protein: 50g, Carb: 60g, Fat 10g

6.3 Spicy Salmon Bowl

Preparation Time: 20 mins

Cooking Time: 1 hr

Servings: 4

Ingredients

For the salmon

- Soy sauce (low sodium), 1/3 cups

- Olive oil (extra-virgin), 1/3 cups

- Chili garlic sauce, 1/4 cup

- Lime juice, 1

- Honey, 2 tbsp

- Garlic (minced), 4 cloves

- Salmon fillets, 4 oz.

For the quick pickled cucumbers

- Rice wine vinegar or rice vinegar, 1/2 cups

- Granulated sugar, 1 tbsp.

- Kosher salt, 1 tsp.

- Sesame oil (toasted), 2 tsp.

- Persian cucumbers (thinly sliced), 3

For the spicy mayo

- Mayonnaise,1/2 cups

- Sriracha, 2 tbsp.

- Sesame oil (toasted), 2 tsp.

For the bowls

- Cooked rice

- Avocado (sliced), 1

- Carrot (shredded), 1 medium

- Red onion (finely sliced), 1/2

- Cilantro leaves, frayed

- Sesame seeds

Steps

1. Making salmon Set the oven to 350 degrees and cover a large baking tray with foil. Mix the olive oil, soy sauce, chili garlic sauce, lemon zest, honey, & garlic in a medium bowl. To mix, add the salmon and gently toss.

2. Place fish on the prepared baking sheet, & bake for 20 to 25 minutes, or till salmon is fork-delicate.

3. Make preserved cucumbers in the interim: Add vinegar, sugar, & salt to a basin or jar that can be microwaved, and then heat for about 2 minutes, or until the sugar and salt have completely dissolved. Sesame oil is stirred in, then cucumbers are added and mixed. Until ready to use, cover with a tight-fitting lid/plastic wrap.

4. Make spicy mayo by mixing mayonnaise, Sriracha, & sesame oil in a small bowl.

5. Create bowls: In four dishes, divide the rice. Add salmon, pickled cucumbers, avocados, red onion, carrots, cilantro, and sesame seeds as garnishes. Add a drizzle of hot mayo.

Nutritional Serving

60 Cal, Protein: 24g, Carb: 12g, Fat 3g

6.4 Green Shakshuka

Preparation Time: 10 mins

Cooking Time: 35 mins

Servings: 3

Ingredients

- Fresh tomatillos (husks removed), 1 lb.

- Olive oil (extra-virgin), 3 1/2 tbsp.

- Kosher salt

- Swiss chard, 1 large bunch

- Onion (chopped), 1 medium

- jalapeño (minced), 1

- Garlic (minced), 3 cloves

- Black pepper (freshly ground)

- Parsley (roughly chopped), 1/2 c.

- Cilantro (roughly chopped), 1/2 cups

- Eggs, 6 large

- Avocado (sliced), 1

- Cotija cheese

- Crusty bread or warm tortillas, for serving

Steps

1. Set the oven to 450 degrees and cover a large baking tray with foil. Trim tomatillos into quarters after thorough rinsing. Toss with 1/2 tablespoon oil and salt on the prepared baking sheet. Tomatillos should be roasted for 20 minutes, rotating them halfway through, until they are softened and beginning to brown slightly. Remove from oven & lower temperature to 325 degrees.

2. Prepare Swiss chard: While waiting, separate the chard stems from the leaves, saving half of the stems. By stacking four to five leaves and firmly rolling them, finely cut the leaves as you work in groups. Vertically slice the roll thinly, then cut the leafy pieces. Separate stems from chard leaves and finely chop them.

3. 2 tablespoons of oil should be heated over medium in a large oven-safe skillet. Cook chard stems, onion, & jalapeno, if using, for five to seven minutes, or until softened and golden. Add the garlic and simmer for 1 minute, or until fragrant.

4. Chard leaves should be added to the skillet in stages, with each batch getting a little time to simmer and decrease before the next batch is added. Until completely wilted, cook greens for five min. Add salt and pepper to taste. Blend the sauce by combining the tomatillos (roasted), herbs, remaining 1 tbsp of oil, & 1 cup of water in a blender while the greens are cooking. When the sauce is smooth, add it to the chard mixture.

5. Heat should be turned down once the sauce reaches a mild boil. Six properly spaced wells can be made in the boiling sauce using a wooden spoon. Add a pinch of salt n pepper to each well after carefully cracking an egg into it. Pan should be taken out of the oven.

6. Bake eggs: Bake eggs for 10 to 13 minutes, or until whites are barely set and yolks still are runny.

7. Served with warm tortilla chips or crusty toast and garnished with cheese, cilantro, and pieces of avocado.

Nutritional Serving

90 Cal, Protein: 45g, Carb: 60g, Fat 31g

6.5 Coconut Ranch Kale Salad

Preparation Time: 20 mins

Cooking Time: 50 mins

Servings: 3

Ingredients

For coconut ranch

- Coconut milk, 1/4 cups

- Vegan mayonnaise, 1/4 cup

- Parsley (freshly chopped), 1 tbsp

- Chives (freshly chopped), 1 tbsp

- Dill (freshly chopped), 2 tsp

- Garlic powder, 1/2 tsp

- Onion powder, 1/4 tsp

- Pinch cayenne pepper

- Kosher salt

- Black pepper (freshly ground)

For salad:

- Sweet potato, 1 large (cut in 1/4")

- Olive oil (extra-virgin), divided 1 tbsp

- Chili powder (divided), 1 1/2 tsp

- Kosher salt

- Black pepper (freshly ground)

- Chickpeas (drained & rinsed), 1 (15-oz.) Can

- Bunch curly kale (washed and dried), 1 large

- Avocado (thinly sliced)

- Vegan parmesan (shaved)

Steps

1. Mayonnaise and coconut milk should be combined in a small bowl. Include herbs, garlic, onion, and a dash of cayenne. Salt & pepper to taste after combining and stirring. Keep chilled until you're ready to use.

2. 400° oven preheat. On a sizable baking sheet, arrange the sweet potatoes. Drizzle with 1 tbsp oil & season with salt, pepper, and 1 teaspoon chili powder. Spread potato pieces out in an equal layer after tossing to coat.

3. Bake for 35 to 40 minutes or until the bottoms are beginning to crisp.

4. Place chickpeas on a medium baking sheet after patting them dry with a paper towel. Bake for 30 minutes, or until crisp and dried out.

5. Place chickpeas in a separate bowl while they are still heated. Add the final 2 tablespoons of oil and the final 1/2 teaspoon of chili powder. Add salt and pepper, toss to incorporate, and season to taste.

6. On a chopping board, place the dry kale and coarsely slice it into bite-sized pieces. Put it in a large bowl. With a generous amount of salt added, rub the kale with your fingers for approximately a minute to help the salt absorb.

7. Sweet potatoes, chickpeas, avocados, & parmesan are good additions to kale. To serve, drizzle with coconut ranch.

Nutritional Serving

60 Cal, Protein: 24g, Carb: 12g, Fat 3g

6.6 Niçoise Salad

Preparation Time: 10 mins

Cooking Time: 40 mins

Servings: 4

Ingredients

For salad

- Kosher salt

- Eggs, 4 large

- Green beans (trimmed), 1/2 lb.

- Small potatoes, 1/2 lb.

- Tuna (packed in olive oil), 16 oz.

- Persian cucumbers, 3 (divided into 1/2" rounds)

- Black olives (Kalamata), 1/2 c.

- Anchovy fillets (packed in oil), 8

- Capers (drained), 2 tbsp.

- Basil leaves, for garnish

For dressing

- Olive oil (extra-virgin), 1/3 cups

- Sherry vinegar, 3 tbsp.

- Oil from canned or jarred tuna, 2 tbsp.

- Garlic (minced or grated), 1 clove

- Dijon mustard, 1 tbsp.

- Honey, 1 tsp.

- Black pepper (freshly ground)

Steps

1. In a medium bowl, set up an ice bath, then over high heat, bring a small pot of water to the boil. Use a spatula to delicately drop the eggs into water while the heat is reduced to a low boil. Using a slotted spoon, move the eggs to an ice bucket to chill after cooking for 8 minutes. Reserving the water while turning off the heat

2. Make dressing in the interim: In a medium bowl, whisk together all the dressing ingredients. Add salt and pepper to taste.

3. Another ice bath should be made in a medium basin. Bring the water in the pot back to the boil over high heat with a generous spoonful of salt. Add the green beans and simmer for 3 to 5 minutes, or until they are brilliant green and barely soft.

4. After cooling off in an ice bath, move to a fresh kitchen towel or some paper towels. After saving the ice bath, pat the green beans dry.

5. Potatoes should be added to boiling water & cooked for 15 minutes or until tender. Drain.

6. Hard-boiled eggs should be peeled and cut in half, as should boiled potatoes. Break tuna into big flakes and drain any residual oil (preserving if wanted).

7. To serve: Distribute the eggs, potatoes, green beans, tuna, cucumbers, & olives among the four big dishes. If used, place one anchovy fillet on every side of an egg.

8. Capers should be added on top, followed by a dressing drizzle and salt and pepper. Basil leaves, and extra dressing should be served as garnish.

Nutritional Serving

50 Cal, Protein: 15g, Carb: 20g, Fat 3.4g

6.7 Burrata Salad

Preparation Time: 10 mins

Cooking Time: 40 mins

Servings: 4

Ingredients

- Beefsteak or heirloom tomatoes (sliced), 3 lb.

- Shallot (finely chopped), 1

- Flaky sea salt

- Black pepper (freshly ground)

- Olive oil (extra-virgin), 2 tbsp

- Red wine vinegar, 2 tbsp

- Panko breadcrumbs, 1/3 cups

- Fresh basil (chopped), 1 tbsp.

- Fresh chives (chopped), 1 tbsp.

- Balls burrata (drained & at room temperature), 2 (4 oz.)

- Crusty bread

Steps

1. Toss tomatoes & shallot on a baking sheet with a rim and season with 1 teaspoon. sea salt & 1 teaspoon. Black pepper. Pour vinegar and oil over top. Allow it settle for 30

   minutes or more, or until tomatoes have shed their juice and shallots have softened.

2. Toast panko for about 2 minutes over low heat, tossing regularly, until golden brown. Place in a compact bowl.

3. Tomatoes are stacked on a big dish. Shallot juices should be drizzled on top.

4. Add panko, 2 teaspoons of basil, and 2 teaspoons of chives. Place the burrata in the middle of the tomatoes, then break it open using your hands. Add the final 1 tsp. of basil & 1 tsp. of chives, along with sea salt and black pepper. Serve alongside bread.

Nutritional Serving

60 Cal, Protein: 24g, Carb: 12g, Fat 3g

6.8 Greek Salmon Salad

Preparation Time: 20 mins

Cooking Time: 50 mins

Servings: 4

Ingredients

For the salmon

- Salmon, 1 lb.

- Kosher salt

- black pepper

- red pepper flakes (Pinch crushed)

- lemon Juice, 1/2

- olive oil (extra-virgin), 1 tbsp

- garlic, 1 clove

- freshly dill (chopped), 1 tbsp

For the dressing

- Greek yogurt, 1/2 cups

- Tahini, 2 tbsp

- lemon Juice, 1/2

- warm water, 2 tbsp

- Kosher salt

- black pepper (Freshly ground)

For the salad

- Baby spinach, 5 oz.

- Head romaine (chopped), 1

- Persian cucumber (sliced), 1

- Red bell pepper (sliced), 1

- Cherry tomatoes (halved), 1 cup

- Kalamata olives (pitted and halved), 1/2 cup

- avocado (sliced), 1

- Red onions (pickled), 1/2 cup

- Crumbled feta, 1/2 cup

- Dill (freshly chopped)

- Lemon wedges

Steps

1. Set a small baking tray in the oven at 350 degrees and line it with foil. Add salt, pepper, & a dash of red pepper flakes to the salmon before placing it on a piece of foil.

2. Combine lime juice, oil, garlic, & dill in a small bowl. Add to the salmon.

3. About 35 minutes into baking, the salmon should be fork-tender, and the internal temperature should be 145°.

4. In the meantime, prepare the dressing by mixing the yogurt, tahini, and lemon juice in a medium bowl. Pour warm water in, then whisk to liquefy. For a thinner dressing with the required consistency, add additional water or lemon juice. Add salt and pepper to taste.

5. Salad construction: Combine the cucumber, romaine, spinach, bell pepper, tomatoes, & olives. Use a fork to break up the salmon into big pieces before adding it to the salad. Add feta, pickled onions, and avocado as garnish. Serve with dressing & lemon wedges after adding the dill garnish.

Nutritional Serving

60 Cal, Protein: 24g, Carb: 12g, Fat 3g

6.9 Butternut Squash Curry

Preparation Time: 15 mins

Cooking Time: 40 mins

Servings: 4

Ingredients

- Peeled, seeded, & large chunks of butternut squash, 1 large (about 2 1/2 lb.)

- Neutral oil (divided), 5 tbsp.

- Kosher salt

- Red onion (coarsely chopped), 1 large

- Garlic (minced), 5 cloves

- Curry powder, 2 tbsp

- Coconut milk (full-fat), 2 (13.5-oz.) Cans

- Bunch of curly kale (roughly chopped), 1 large (about 6.5 oz.)

- Lime juice, 1

- Fresh parsley (chopped), 1/4 cup

- Sunflower seeds, 1/4 cup

- Cooked rice

Steps

1. 400° oven preheat. Combine squash with 3 tbsp oil and salt in a large bowl. Squash should be arranged in a uniform layer on a baking sheet with a rim. Roast for 35 to 40 minutes, or until fork-tender and golden brown.

2. The remaining 2 tablespoons of oil should be heated in a big pan over medium-high heat in the meantime. Add the onion, add the salt, & simmer for 8 minutes while stirring regularly. Medium-low heat should be used. Add the garlic and stir-fry for approximately a minute, or until fragrant. Stirring often, add the curry powder and continue cooking. Add coconut milk and raise heat to medium. Add the kale after bringing to a boil, then salt to taste. Cook for approximately 3 minutes, stirring periodically, until wilted and soft. As soon as the squash begins to roast, turn off the heat.

3. Stir together the squash & lime juice in the skillet.

4. Give each bowl of rice. Spread out the squash mixture and sprinkle the parsley & sunflower seeds on top.

5. Squash may be roasted a day in advance. Transfer to the an airtight jar and refrigerate after allowing to cool.

Nutritional Serving

189 Cal, Protein: 15g, Carb: 110g, Fat 56g

6.10 Balsamic Basil Chicken

Preparation Time: 10 mins

Cooking Time: 55 mins

Servings: 4

Ingredients

- Olive oil (extra-virgin), 1/4 cup

- Balsamic vinegar, 3 tbsp

- Dijon mustard, 1 tbsp

- Bone-in chicken thighs (skin-on), 2 lb.

- Kosher salt

- Black pepper (freshly ground)

- Zucchini, 1 large

- Cherry tomatoes (halved), 1 pt.

- Parmesan (freshly grated)

- Basil (thinly sliced)

Steps

1. Mix 1/4 cup vinegar, olive oil, & mustard in a big basin. Chicken thighs should be added and coated. For thirty min or up to four hours, cover and chill.

2. Set the oven to 425°. Heat the remaining oil in a large oven-safe pan over medium-high heat. Chicken should be seasoned all over with salt n pepper after shaking off excess marinade. Add into hot pan with skin-side down and cook for 6 minutes or until brown and charred. About 6 minutes after flipping the chicken, grill the opposite side until charred.

3. Around the chicken, scatter the tomatoes and zucchini. Vegetables should be salted and peppered before being added to the oven. Bake for a further 15 minutes, or until a thermometer put into the thickest portion of the chicken registers 165°.

4. Before serving, add basil and Parmesan as garnish.

Nutritional Serving

150 Cal, Protein: 52.3g, Carb: 10g, Fat 26g

6.11 Vegan "Scallops" with Succotash

Preparation Time: 15 mins

Cooking Time: 35 mins

Servings: 4

Ingredients

FOR "SCALLOPS"

- White miso, 2 tbsp

- Mirin, 2 tbsp

- Low-sodium tamari or soy sauce, 2 tbsp

- King trumpet mushrooms caps, 6 large (1 ½ pound)

- Canola oil, 2 tbsp

FOR CORN SUCCOTASH

- Fresh ears of corn (shucked), 4

- Canola oil, 1 tbsp

- Vegan butter, 1 tbsp

- Red onion, 1/2 medium

- Red bell pepper (seeded), 1 medium

- Garlic (finely chopped), 3 cloves

- Almond milk (unsweetened), 1 cup

- Snap peas, 6 oz.

- Sesame oil (toasted), 1 tsp

- Smoked paprika, 1/4 tsp

- Kosher salt

- Freshly ground black pepper

- Scallions (chopped), 2

- Toasted almonds (chopped), 1/2 cup

Steps

Make "scallops"

1. Miso, mirin, & soy sauce are combined inside a small bowl and whisked until combined. Into a small baking dish, pour marinade. Mushroom stems should be added to the marinade and coated. Place the cut side of the stems on the bottom. Scallops should be marinated for at least 30 mins & up to overnight in the refrigerator.

2. Make corn succotash in the interim: Remove the kernels from the corn with a chef's knife (you should obtain around 2 12 cups of kernels) and put them in a basin. Cobs should be placed standing up inside a medium dish. Scrape any liquid still on the cob into to the bowl using back of a knife. Cobs are discarded, and juice is kept.

3. Oil should be heated over medium heat in a large, heavy-bottomed pan for scallops. Add "scallops" in a single layer, cut side down. Cook for about 4 minutes total, turning halfway through until browned on both sides. Place on a platter.

4. Remove and discard any leftover oil in the skillet. Use paper towels to clean the skillet.

Make succotash

1. Stir fry pan back over medium heat. Add butter and canola oil. Add bell pepper and onion when the butter has melted. Cook for 2 minutes, stirring periodically, until the vegetables begin to soften. Add the chopped mushroom caps & garlic, and simmer for an additional two minutes while stirring.

2. Add the corn kernels, snap peas, sesame oil, paprika, and any saved corn juice to the almond milk mixture. Stir in the salt and pepper after seasoning. Simmer for a while.

3. Place scallops in the combination of corn and cover the pan. Simmer for about 5 minutes, or until the scallops, corn, & snap peas are crisp-tender.

4. Put some in dishes and sprinkle almonds and scallions on top.

Nutritional Serving

180 Cal, Protein: 80g, Carb: 74.3g, Fat 16g

6.12 Best-Ever Farro Salad

Preparation Time: 10 mins

Cooking Time: 1 hr

Servings: 4

Ingredients

- Farro (whole grain), 1 cup

- Vegetable broth (low sodium), 2 cups

- Kosher salt, 1 1/2 tsp.

- Bay leaf, 1

- Shallot (very thinly sliced), 1 large

- Extra virgin olive oil, 1/3 cup

- Apple cider vinegar, 3 tbsp

- Dijon mustard, 1 tbsp

- Honey, 2 tsp

- Black pepper (freshly ground)

- Arugula (lightly packed), 2 cups

- Green apple (chopped), 1

- Parmesan (shaved), 1/2 cup

- Basil (freshly chopped), 1/4 cup

- Parsley (freshly chopped), 2 tbsp

- Toasted pecans (roughly chopped), 1/4 cup

Steps

1. Combine the salt, vegetable broth, farro, & bay leaf in a medium saucepan. Cook for about 30 minutes, stirring regularly, until the farro is soft and there is no longer any broth after bringing to a boil. Transfer the cooked farro to a large basin to cool.

2. Make fried shallots in the interim by combining oil and shallots inside a small saucepan on a medium heat. Reduce the heat to medium-low & continue cooking the shallots, stirring periodically, for 15 to 20 minutes after they start to boil. With a slotted spoon, remove the shallots from the oil and lay them on a dish covered with paper towels before salting them. Cool the oil.

3. To make the dressing, mix the chilled olive oil with the vinegar, mustard, honey, and salt and pepper in a medium bowl.

4. Prepared apple, crispy shallots, arugula, farro, parmesan, basil, parsley, & nuts should all be combined in the salad. Over the salad, drizzle the dressing & toss to coat.

Nutritional Serving

20.2 Cal, Protein: 9.3g, Carb: 15g, Fat 6g

6.13 Zucchini Bolognese

Preparation Time: 10 mins

Cooking Time: 4 hrs 10 mins

Servings: 4

Ingredients

- olive oil (extra-virgin), 1 tbsp

- white onion (chopped), 1 medium

- zucchini (chopped), 5 medium

- water, 1/2 cup

- chicken bouillon cube, 1

- Kosher salt

- black pepper (Freshly ground)

- rigatoni, 3/4 lb.

- lemon Juice, 1/2

- Parmesan (freshly grated), 1 c.

- Pinch red pepper flakes

Steps

1. Heat oil in a big saucepan over a medium heat. Add the onion and simmer for about 6 minutes, or until tender. Add the water, bouillon cube, and zucchini and stir. Add salt and pepper to taste.

2. Turn down the heat and cover the saucepan. The zucchini should disappear after 4 hours of cooking and frequent stirring. It'll be mushy, which is nice.

3. Bring a big saucepan of salt water to a boil whenever the sauce is now almost done. According to the directions on the package, add the pasta and simmer until al dente. Add to saucepan with zucchini after draining.

4. Pasta should be properly combined after being added with the Parmesan cheese, lemon juice, and pepper flakes. Serve with more Parmesan on top.

Nutritional Serving

78 Cal, Protein: 64g, Carb: 42g, Fat 19g

6.14 Avocado Chicken Salad

Preparation Time: 25 mins

Cooking Time: 10 mins

Servings: 4

Ingredients

- Chicken breasts (boneless & skinless), 2

- Avocados (cubed), 2

- Mango (cubed), 1 small

- Grape tomatoes (quartered), 1 cup

- Frozen or fresh corn, 1/2 cup

- Red onion (thinly sliced), 1/4

For dressing

- Lime juice, 1/4 cup

- Olive oil extra-virgin, 3 tbsp

- Cilantro freshly chopped, 2 tbsp

- Minced jalapeno, 1 tbsp

- Honey, 2 tsp

- Kosher salt

- Black pepper (freshly ground)

Steps

1. To make the dressing, mix the ingredients in a medium bowl & season with salt & pepper.

2. Combine the salad ingredients and dressing in a big bowl. After giving the salad a little toss to evenly distribute the dressing, add salt and pepper to taste.

Nutritional Serving

88 Cal, Protein: 26g, Carb: 61.2g, Fat 12g

6.15 Thai-Inspired Grilled Cauliflower Steaks

Preparation Time: 15 mins

Cooking Time: 15 mins

Servings: 2

Ingredients

- Head cauliflower, 1 large

- Olive oil extra-virgin, 1 tbsp

- Kosher salt

- Black pepper (freshly ground)

- Cilantro (freshly chopped), 1/4 cup

- Shallot (finely diced), 1 small

- Clove garlic (minced), 1 small

- Brown sugar, 1 tbsp

- Fish sauce or soy sauce, 1 tbsp

- Red pepper flakes (crushed), 1/2 tsp

- Lime juice & zest, 1

- Salted peanuts (chopped), 1/4 cup

Steps

1. Grill to a medium heat. Cut the cauliflower into 1-inch-thick "steaks" by placing the stem-side down on a cutting board. Rub olive oil all over & sprinkle salt and pepper on both sides.

2. Grill covered cauliflower for 8 minutes on each side or until charred and soft.

3. In the meantime, combine cilantro, shallot, ginger, brown sugar, sauce, red pepper flakes, & the juice and zest of one lime in a small bowl.

4. Place the cooked cauliflower on a serving plate, top with sauce, then top with peanuts.

Nutritional Serving

66 Cal, Protein: 15g, Carb: 18g, Fat 6g

6.16 Sweet Corn Shrimp & Rice Skillet

Preparation Time: 15 mins

Cooking Time: 45 mins

Servings: 2

Ingredients

- Basmati rice, 1/2 cups

- Green onions (divided), 1 bunch

- Red bell pepper (chopped), 1 medium

- Garlic cloves, 6

- White miso, 4 tbsp

- Ginger (thinly sliced), 2" piece

- Turmeric powder, 1 1/4 tsp

- Kosher salt, 1 tsp

- Granulated sugar, 1 tsp

- Ground cayenne pepper, 1/2 tsp

- Olive oil extra-virgin, 4 tbsp

- Shrimp (peeled & cleaned), 1/2 lb.

- Black pepper, freshly ground

- Water, 3/4 cups

- Frozen corn (rinsed & drained), 1 cup

- Lime wedges

Steps

1. After thoroughly rinsing the rice until the water is clear, place it in a medium bowl & fill it with water. Set the oven to 375 degrees.

2. Four green onions should have their roots and ends cut off and be coarsely chopped. Add the bell pepper, Five roughly sliced garlic cloves, soy, ginger, 1 tsp turmeric, salt, sugar, and, if needed, cayenne pepper to the food processor or blender along with the chopped scallions. Once all ingredients are well combined and finely chopped, carefully dribble in 3 tablespoons of extra virgin olive oil while running the food processor and blender. Mixture should be smooth after blending.

3. After being dried off, add the shrimp to a small bowl. Sprinkle salt and pepper over the mixture before adding the remaining turmeric and chopped garlic. In a 12-inch oven-safe skillet, heat the last tablespoon of oil over medium heat. Add the shrimp and cook for two to three minutes per side, or until opaque. Put fried shrimp into a bowl that is just large enough to hold them, then cover with a plate to keep them warm.

4. Add puree after heating skillet one more. Cook for 8 to 10 minutes, often stirring, on medium-high heat, until the paste has darkened and the liquid has evaporated. (When the oil begins to break from the paste, it's finished.

5. Heat should be reduced to medium. Add water and whisk until smooth. Pour any cooking fluids from of the shrimp into to the skillet along with the corn and rice, using the spatula to prevent the shrimp from dropping in. (Make sure shrimp are covered.)

6. Stir everything together, then heat mixture to a simmer. Put in the oven and securely use a lid or a sheet pan. Bake for 23 to 25 minutes, or until all liquid has been absorbed and the rice is soft. Slice the remaining green onions very thinly for garnish.

7. With a fork, fluff the rice before scooping it into serving bowls. Serve with lemon wedges just on side and top over cooked shrimp & green onions.

Nutritional Serving

60 Cal, Protein: 12g, Carb: 19g, Fat 12g

6.17 Cilantro-Lime Shrimp Wraps

Preparation Time: 10 mins

Cooking Time: 15 mins

Servings: 4

Ingredients

- Medium shrimp (peeled & deveined), 1 lb.

- Ground cumin, 2 tsp

- Chili powder, 1 tsp

- Lime juice, 1

- Cilantro (freshly chopped), 2 tbsp

- Minced garlic, 2 cloves

- Olive oil extra-virgin, 3 tbsp.

- Kosher salt

- Black pepper (freshly ground)

- Romaine lettuce

- Avocado (thinly sliced), 1

- Sour cream, 1/4 cup

Steps

1. Combine the shrimp, cumin, lemon zest, cilantro, garlic, & 2 tablespoons oil in a large bowl. Add salt and pepper to taste. Stir to blend, then let sit for ten minutes in the refrigerator.

2. The final tablespoon of oil should be heated in a big pan over medium heat. Add shrimp and marinade; cook for 2 minutes on each side or until pink.

3. To assemble the wraps, combine the lettuce with the shrimp, avocado, sour cream, and cilantro.

Nutritional Serving

51 Cal, Protein: 13g, Carb: 24.3g, Fat 19g

6.18 West African-Inspired Chicken & Peanut Stew

Preparation Time: 30 mins

Cooking Time: 1 hr 30 mins

Servings: 7

Ingredients

- Black pepper (freshly ground), 1 tsp

- Ground cumin,1/2 tsp

- Ground cardamom, 1/4 tsp

- Kosher salt (divided), 4 tsp

- Ginger (peeled &minced), 1 (2") piece

- 4 cloves garlic, minced, divided

- Neutral or peanut oil, 3 tbsp.

- Boneless & skinless chicken thighs, 1 1/2 lb.

- Onion (finely chopped), 1 medium

- Peeled carrots, 2 medium

- Habanero or scotch bonnet pepper Chile (halved), 1

- Thyme leaves (chopped fresh), 2 tbsp

- Tomato paste, 2 tbsp

- Beef steak or Roma tomatoes (finely chopped), 1 1/4 lb.

- Peanut butter (smooth), 1 cup

- Chicken broth (low sodium), 4 cups

- Sweet potato chopped, 1 medium

- Fish sauce, 2 tbsp

- White rice cooked, 3 cups

- Roasted peanuts chopped, 3/4 cup

Steps

1. Combine pepper, cardamom, cumin, & 2 tsp. Salt in a small bowl. Combine 2 1/2 teaspoons of spice mix, half a clove each of ginger and garlic, and 1 tablespoon of oil in a medium bowl. With paper towels, dry the chicken, then add it to the dish and toss to coat. Allow chicken to rest for at least 15 minutes at room temperature or for up to 2 hours in the refrigerator.

2. Heat the final 2 tablespoons of oil in a big Dutch oven or saucepan over medium heat. Chicken should be cooked in a single layer, five to six minutes per side, till a golden-brown coating begins to develop. Placing the chicken on a platter.

3. Cook onion, carrot, & remaining spice mix in the same pan for approximately 5 minutes, stirring regularly and scraping up any browned pieces from the bottom of the pan. Stirring constantly, sauté the remaining ginger & garlic with the pepper for about a minute or until fragrant. Cook the tomato paste for about 4 minutes, stirring often as it darkens in color. Cook, stirring regularly & going to break up tomatoes with such a wooden spoon, till mostly broken down, approximately 20 minutes. Add diced tomatoes & 2 tsp. Salt.

4. Mix 1 cup of broth and the peanut butter in a big bowl or cup until combined. One cup at the a time, whisk in the remaining cup of broth until thoroughly incorporated. Stir together the potatoes and broth mixture before adding to the saucepan. Simmer for about 30 minutes, stirring periodically, until potatoes are fork-tender and the soup has thickened over medium-low heat.

5. Chicken should be cut into bite-sized pieces. Return the chicken to the pot after removing the pepper. Stir in the fish sauce and cook the chicken thoroughly.

6. Give each bowl of rice. Over rice, spoon the soup and sprinkle with peanuts & thyme.

7. Stew can be prepared five days in advance. After transferring, seal the container tightly. Chill or freeze for up to three months.

Nutritional Serving

94 Cal, Protein: 26g, Carb: 12g, Fat 2g

6.19 Garlicky Lemon Mahi-Mahi

Preparation Time: 10 mins

Cooking Time: 20 mins

Servings: 2

Ingredients

- Butter, 3 tbsp

- Olive oil extra-virgin, 2 tbsp

- Mahi-mahi fillets, 4 (4-oz.)

- Kosher salt

- Black pepper (freshly ground)

- Asparagus, 1 lb.

- Minced garlic, 3 cloves

- Red pepper flakes (crushed), 1/4 tsp.

- lemon (sliced), 1

- Lemon zest & juice, 1

- Parsley freshly chopped, 1 tbsp

Steps

1. Melt one tablespoon of butter and one tablespoon of olive oil in a large pan over medium heat. Mahi-mahi should be added after adding salt and pepper. Cook for four to five minutes on each side or until golden. Place on a platter.

2. Add remaining 1 tbsp oil to the skillet. Cook the asparagus for 2 to 4 minutes or until it is tender. Add salt and pepper, then move to a platter.

3. Add the final 2 tablespoons of butter to the skillet. Once melted, whisk in the garlic & red pepper flakes, cooking for 1 minute or until aromatic. Then, add the lemon zest, juice, & parsley. Remove from the heat, then add the mahi-mahi, asparagus, and sauce back to the pan.

4. Before serving, add additional parsley as a garnish.

Nutritional Serving

101 Cal, Protein: 15g, Carb: 24g, Fat 10.3g

6.20 Jerk Tofu Grain Bowls

Preparation Time: 25 mins

Cooking Time: 2 hrs

Servings: 4

Ingredients

For the fried plantains

- Ripe plantains, 2 large

- For frying vegetable oil

- Kosher salt

For the cabbage carrot slaw

- Red cabbage shredded, 1 small

- Carrot sliced into matchsticks, 1 large

- Kosher salt, 1 tsp

- Olive oil extra-virgin, 2 tbsp

- Apple cider vinegar, 2 tbsp

- Lime juice, 1

- Honey, 1/2 tbsp

- Dijon mustard, 1/2 tbsp

- Kosher salt

- Black pepper (freshly ground)

For the quick rice & peas

- Red kidney beans (undrained), 1 (15-ounce) can

- Coconut milk, 1 (7-ounce) can

- Halved scallions, 2

- Allspice berries, 10

- Garlic, 3 cloves

- Scotch bonnet pepper (seeds removed), 1/2

- Sprigs thyme, 2

- Basmati rice, 1 cup

- Kosher salt

For the tofu & bowls

- Onion (roughly chopped), 1 medium

- Scallion roughly chopped, 3

- Piece ginger (roughly chopped), 2 inches

- Scotch bonnet peppers, 2

- sprigs thyme (leaves removed & stems discard), 3

- Freshly ground allspice, 3 tsp

- Soy sauce (low sodium), 1/4 cup

- Apple cider vinegar, 1/4 cup

- Kosher salt

- Black pepper (freshly ground)

- Cinnamon, 1/4 tsp

- Garlic powder, 1 tsp

- Extra firm tofu (drained & pressed), 2 (16-ounce) packages

- Olive oil extra virgin

- Finely chopped cilantro

- Lime wedges

Steps

For the fried plantains

1. Just enough oil should be added to a big skillet to cover the bottom. Heat the oil until it shimmers at medium-high heat. Slices of plantain should be added to the pan inside a single layer, carefully.

2. For six to eight minutes, fry, flipping once halfway through. Remove the plantains to a plate lined with paper towels and sprinkle with salt when they are deep golden brown & easily punctured with a fork.

For the carrot cabbage slaw

1. Combine the cabbage, carrots, and salt in a large bowl and set aside about 15 minutes. To remove the moisture, squeeze a cabbage mixture over a sink.

2. In the meantime, mix the lemon juice, vinegar, olive oil, honey, & mustard in a small bowl. To taste, add salt n pepper to the food. Dress the cabbage with the dressing, then chill.

For the quick rice & peas

1. Add the kidney beans, coconut milk, and 1 cup plus 2 teaspoons water to a medium saucepan set over medium heat. Add thyme, scotch bonnet, garlic, allspice, scallions, and a large amount of salt & black pepper. Bring to a boil, then lower the heat to a simmer, cover, and cook for 20 minutes.

2. Basmati should be thoroughly rinsed in a fine mesh sieve with cold water till the water is clear. Take out the garlic, onions, and spices. If a significant amount of the liquid has evaporated, top it with water to the original level and then bring to a boil. Add the rice, lower the heat to a simmer, and cook it covered for fifteen to twenty minutes or until it is tender.

For the tofu and bowls

1. Add the ginger, scallion, onion, scotch bonnet, thyme, 2 tbsp allspice, soy sauce, and vinegar to a blender or food processor. Blend until a pastry consistency is achieved. In a big bowl, season with salt n pepper & reserve.

2. Slice the tofu into quarters and season with salt, pepper, 1 teaspoon each of allspice, cinnamon, and garlic powder, and 1 teaspoon of allspice. Tofu should be added to the jerk marinade & gently mixed to coat, being careful not to break the pieces. For at least two hours and maybe overnight, cover in plastic wrap and refrigerate.

3. Set a rack inside the top and Centre of your oven and preheat it to 400°F. Lay the tofu slices in a single layer on a baking sheet lined with parchment paper, making sure that some of marinade has clung to the pieces. For 30 minutes, roast the tofu on the Centre rack, turning it occasionally, until the edges are browned, and the jerk spice has slightly darkened. Place the tray on the top rack & broil for 2-3 mins on high or till the tofu starts to sear in spots.

4. In a big bowl, assemble rice, three to four slices of tofu, plantains, & slaw to serve. Lime wedges, cilantro, and a sprinkling of thinly sliced scallions should be used as garnish.

Nutritional Serving

26 Cal, Protein: 16g, Carb: 20g, Fat 3g

6.21 Sweet Potato Salad

Preparation Time: 10 mins

Cooking Time: 30 mins

Servings: 6

Ingredients

- Peeled & cubed sweet potatoes, 3 large (about 2 lb.)

- Red onion thinly sliced, 1 small

- Olive oil (extra-virgin), 2 tbsp.

- Kosher salt

- Black pepper (freshly ground)

- Dried cranberries, 1/2 cup

- Crumbled feta, 1/2 cup

- Freshly chopped parsley, 1/4 cup

For the dressing

- Apple cider vinegar, 2 tbsp

- Dijon mustard, 1 tbsp

- Honey, 1 tbsp

- Ground cumin, 1/2 tsp

- Ground paprika, 1/4 tsp

- Olive oil extra-virgin, 1/4 cup

Steps

1. 400° oven preheat. Sweet potatoes & red onion are tossed in oil and salt and pepper on a wide baking sheet with a rim.

2. Put them in a single layer, spaced out evenly, on the sheet. Bake for about 20 minutes, or until soft. After 10 min of cooling, transfer to a big bowl.

3. Make dressing in the interim: Mix the vinegar, mustard, honey, & spices in a small dish or a moderate liquid measuring cup. Pour the oil in gradually while continuing to whisk to create an emulsion. Add salt and pepper to taste.

4. Sweet potatoes should be mixed with the dressing, feta, parsley, and cranberries. At room temperature or heated, serve.

Nutritional Serving

51 Cal, Protein: 18g, Carb: 20g, Fat 6g

6.22 Honey Mustard Chicken

Preparation Time: 15 mins

Cooking Time: 30 mins

Servings: 4

Ingredients

- Kosher salt

- Honey, 2 tbsp

- Dijon mustard, 1/4 cup

- Grated or minced garlic, 1 clove

- Lime zest, 1/2 tsp

- Cilantro leaves chopped fresh, 1 tbsp.

- Olive oil extra-virgin, 2 tbsp.

- Brussels sprouts, 7 oz.

- Peeled & quartered shallot, 1

- Bone-in & skin-on chicken thighs, 1 1/2 lb.

- Small, sweet potato, 1 (7 oz)

- Jalapeño pepper, 1

- Kosher salt

- Freshly ground black pepper

Steps

1. Place the oven rack in the middle & make the oven upto 425 degrees.

2. Honey, Dijon, garlic, lemon zest, 1 tbsp of cilantro stems, & 1 tsp of oil should all be whisked together in a medium basin. Add the other half of the dressing to a different little bowl. (The chicken will be prepared with this.)

3. The remaining dressing inside the medium dish should be tossed with the Brussels sprouts, shallots, & 1/2 teaspoon salt to evenly cover everything.

4. Each chicken thigh should be placed skin-side down on the chopping board with the superfluous skin flaps spread out. Trim the skin all around edge of the meat so that it protrudes by approximately a half inch. Dry each piece well with a clean towel before seasoning it with a little salt and black pepper on both sides.

5. 1 tbsp of oil should be heated to shimmering condition in a big cast iron pan over medium-high heat. The thighs should be cooked skin-side down for 5 minutes, untouched. Cook for an extra 5 minutes after rotating each piece to make sure the fat is uniformly rendered from the skin. (The skin needs to have a rich golden brown color.) Onto a platter, transfer the chicken. Clean the pan after draining the fat.

6. Mix the sweet potatoes, jalapenos, and last teaspoon of oil in a small bowl. Add a few grinds of pepper and a sprinkle of salt to taste.

7. Once more, over medium heat, add 1 tsp of oil and stir until shimmering.

8. Put the veggies in the pan with the Brussels sprouts on the outside, facing down. Next, arrange the sweet potatoes & jalapenos in a ring. Finally, place the shallots in the Centre, cut side down. With the skin facing up, arrange those chicken thighs on top of sweet potatoes, jalapenos, and shallots. To prevent the Brussels sprouts from heating and becoming too mushy, do not cover the outer layer.

9. After placing the pan in the oven, roast the food there for 15 minutes. The sliced surface of Brussels sprouts should be a rich shade of brown. Pan should be taken out of the oven after the chicken thighs have been brushed with the remaining vinaigrette. (Instead of brushing the marinade on top of every piece of chicken, do so on the underside for additional crispy skin.) After 5 more minutes of roasting, remove it from the oven & sprinkle chopped cilantro on top.

Nutritional Serving

15 Cal, Protein: 2g, Carb: 8g, Fat 3g

6.23 Grilled Honey-Chipotle Salmon Foil Packets with Summer Squash

Preparation Time: 10 mins

Cooking Time: 20 mins

Servings: 4

Ingredients

- Melted butter, 4 tbsp

- Honey, 2 tbsp

- Regular chili powder or chipotle chili powder 1 tbsp

- Minced garlic, 3 cloves

- Kosher salt

- Salmon filets skin-on, 4 (6-oz.)

- Zucchini sliced, 1 medium

- Summer squash sliced, 1

- Red onion sliced, 1 small

- Basil leaves frayed packed, 1/4 cup

- Lime wedges

Steps

1. Grill to a medium-high temperature. Butter, honey, chipotle Chile powder, garlic, and 1/2 teaspoon salt should all be combined in a small bowl.

2. Add 1/4 teaspoon salt to the salmon's surface on both sides. Combine zucchini, summer squash, & red onion in a medium bowl and season with 1/4 teaspoon salt.

3. Place four foil pieces measuring 12" by 16" on flat surface. Fill up 1/2 of the middle of every piece of foil with the veggie mixture before dividing it into foil packets. Salmon should be placed next to vegetables. Distribute the chipotle sauce evenly over the fish and veggies, stirring it together if necessary. To make a package, fold and seal the foil's edges.

4. Cook fish and squash covered on the grill for 11 to 14 minutes, turning packets halfway through. Serve using lime wedges and basil sprigs.

Nutritional Serving

46 Cal, Protein: 10g, Carb: 11g, Fat 6g

61-Day Meal Plan

Week 1

Meal	Mon	Tue	Wed	Thu	Fri	Sat	Sun
Breakfast	Spinach Smoothie	Mango & Kale Smoothie	Green Smoothie	Egg Salad	South Western Waffle	West Coast	Arugula & Avocado Omelet
Lunch	Lettuce Wraps	Veggie Salad & White Bean	Vegan Bistro Lunch Box	Hummus & Veggie Sandwich	Sweet & Savory Hummus Plate	Lettuce Wraps	Special Arugula Omelet
Dinner	Golden Veggie Soup	Beef Balti & Lamb	Apple Soup & Curried Parsnip	Roasted Carrot Soup	Pumpkin Curry Soup	Kale Frittata & Cauliflo	Soup of Vegan Carrot Ginger

						wer	
Snack	Avocado Hummus	Garlic Hummus	Chickpea Snack Salad	Peanut Butter Energy Balls	Mango-Date Energy Bites	Beet Jerky	Rice Cake Sandwich
Salad, Dressing & Appetizer	Grilled Tomatoes	Greek Salmon Salad	Sweet Potato Salad	Honey Mustard Chicken	Spicy Salmon Bowl	Chicken & Wild Rice Soup	Jerk Tofu Grain Bowls

Week 2

Meal	Mon	Tue	Wed	Thu	Fri	Sat	Sun
Breakfast	Egg Salad	Mango & Kale Smoothie	West Coast	Spinach Smoothie	South Western Waffle	Arugula & Avocado Omelet	Green Smoothie
Lunch	Special Arugula Omelet	Vegan Bistro Lunch Box	Veggie Salad & White Bean	Lettuce Wraps	Sweet & Savory Hummus Plate	Hummus & Veggie Sandwich	Lettuce Wraps
Dinner	Kale Frittata & Cauliflower	Soup of Vegan Carrot Ginger	Roasted Carrot Soup	Apple Soup & Curried Parsnip	Pumpkin Curry Soup	Golden Veggie Soup	Beef Balti & Lamb

Snack							
	Rice Cake Sandwich	Garlic Hummus	Chickpea Snack Salad	Mango-Date Energy Bites	Peanut Butter Energy Balls	Beet Jerky	Avocado Hummus
Salad, Dressing & Appetizer	Sweet Potato Salad	Greek Salmon Salad	Chicken & Wild Rice Soup	Jerk Tofu Grain Bowls	Spicy Salmon Bowl	Grilled Tomatoes	Honey Mustard Chicken

Week 3

Meal	Mon	Tue	Wed	Thu	Fri	Sat	Sun
Breakfast	Spinach Smoothie	Mango & Kale Smoothie	Green Smoothie	Egg Salad	South Western Waffle	West Coast	Arugula & Avocado Omelet
Lunch	Lettuce Wraps	Veggie Salad & White Bean	Vegan Bistro Lunch Box	Hummus & Veggie Sandwich	Sweet & Savory Hummus Plate	Lettuce Wraps	Special Arugula Omelet
Dinner	Golden Veggie Soup	Beef Balti & Lamb	Apple Soup & Curried Parsnip	Roasted Carrot Soup	Pumpkin Curry Soup	Kale Frittata & Cauliflower	Soup of Vegan Carrot Ginger

Snack	Avocado Hummus	Garlic Hummus	Chickpea Snack Salad	Peanut Butter Energy Balls	Mango-Date Energy Bites	Beet Jerky	Rice Cake Sandwich
Salad, Dressing & Appetizer	Grilled Tomatoes	Greek Salmon Salad	Sweet Potato Salad	Honey Mustard Chicken	Spicy Salmon Bowl	Chicken & Wild Rice Soup	Jerk Tofu Grain Bowls

Week 4

Meal	Mon	Tue	Wed	Thu	Fri	Sat	Sun
Breakfast	Egg Salad	Mango & Kale Smoothie	West Coast	Spinach Smoothie	South Western Waffle	Arugula & Avocado Omelet	Green Smoothie
Lunch	Special Arugula Omelet	Vegan Bistro Lunch Box	Veggie Salad & White Bean	Lettuce Wraps	Sweet & Savory Hummus Plate	Hummus & Veggie Sandwich	Lettuce Wraps
Dinner	Kale Frittata & Cauliflower	Soup of Vegan Carrot Ginger	Roasted Carrot Soup	Apple Soup & Curried Parsnip	Pumpkin Curry Soup	Golden Veggie Soup	Beef Balti & Lamb

Snack	Rice Cake Sandwich	Garlic Hummus	Chickpea Snack Salad	Mango-Date Energy Bites	Peanut Butter Energy Balls	Beet Jerky	Avocado Hummus
Salad, Dressing & Appetizer	Sweet Potato Salad	Greek Salmon Salad	Chicken & Wild Rice Soup	Jerk Tofu Grain Bowls	Spicy Salmon Bowl	Grilled Tomatoes	Honey Mustard Chicken

Week 5

Meal	Mon	Tue	Wed	Thu	Fri	Sat	Sun
Breakfast	Spinach Smoothie	Mango & Kale Smoothie	Green Smoothie	Egg Salad	South Western Waffle	West Coast	Arugula & Avocado Omelet
Lunch	Lettuce Wraps	Veggie Salad & White Bean	Vegan Bistro Lunch Box	Hummus & Veggie Sandwich	Sweet & Savory Hummus Plate	Lettuce Wraps	Special Arugula Omelet
Dinner	Golden Veggie Soup	Beef Balti & Lamb	Apple Soup & Curried Parsnip	Roasted Carrot Soup	Pumpkin Curry Soup	Kale Frittata & Cauliflower	Soup of Vegan Carrot Ginger

Snack	Avocado Hummus	Garlic Hummus	Chickpea Snack Salad	Peanut Butter Energy Balls	Mango-Date Energy Bites	Beet Jerky	Rice Cake Sandwich
Salad, Dressing & Appetizer	Grilled Tomatoes	Greek Salmon Salad	Sweet Potato Salad	Honey Mustard Chicken	Spicy Salmon Bowl	Chicken & Wild Rice Soup	Jerk Tofu Grain Bowls

Week 6

Meal	Mon	Tue	Wed	Thu	Fri	Sat	Sun
Breakfast	Egg Salad	Mango & Kale Smoothie	West Coast	Spinach Smoothie	South Western Waffle	Arugula & Avocado Omelet	Green Smoothie
Lunch	Special Arugula Omelet	Vegan Bistro Lunch Box	Veggie Salad & White Bean	Lettuce Wraps	Sweet & Savory Hummus Plate	Hummus & Veggie Sandwich	Lettuce Wraps
Dinner	Kale Frittata & Cauliflower	Soup of Vegan Carrot Ginger	Roasted Carrot Soup	Apple Soup & Curried Parsnip	Pumpkin Curry Soup	Golden Veggie Soup	Beef Balti & Lamb

Snack	Rice Cake Sandwich	Garlic Hummus	Chickpea Snack Salad	Mango-Date Energy Bites	Peanut Butter Energy Balls	Beet Jerky	Avocado Hummus
Salad, Dressing & Appetizer	Sweet Potato Salad	Greek Salmon Salad	Chicken & Wild Rice Soup	Jerk Tofu Grain Bowls	Spicy Salmon Bowl	Grilled Tomatoes	Honey Mustard Chicken

Week 7

Meal	Mon	Tue	Wed	Thu	Fri	Sat	Sun
Breakfast	Spinach Smoothie	Mango & Kale Smoothie	Green Smoothie	Egg Salad	South Western Waffle	West Coast	Arugula & Avocado Omelet
Lunch	Lettuce Wraps	Veggie Salad & White Bean	Vegan Bistro Lunch Box	Hummus & Veggie Sandwich	Sweet & Savory Hummus Plate	Lettuce Wraps	Special Arugula Omelet
Dinner	Golden Veggie Soup	Beef Balti & Lamb	Apple Soup & Curried Parsnip	Roasted Carrot Soup	Pumpkin Curry Soup	Kale Frittata & Cauliflower	Soup of Vegan Carrot Ginger

Snack						
Avocado Hummus	Garlic Hummus	Chickpea Snack Salad	Peanut Butter Energy Balls	Mango-Date Energy Bites	Beet Jerky	Rice Cake Sandwich

Salad, Dressing & Appetizer						
Grilled Tomatoes	Greek Salmon Salad	Sweet Potato Salad	Honey Mustard Chicken	Spicy Salmon Bowl	Chicken & Wild Rice Soup	Jerk Tofu Grain Bowls

Week 8

Meal	Mon	Tue	Wed	Thu	Fri	Sat	Sun
Breakfast	Egg Salad	Mango & Kale Smoothie	West Coast	Spinach Smoothie	South Western Waffle	Arugula & Avocado Omelet	Green Smoothie
Lunch	Special Arugula Omelet	Vegan Bistro Lunch Box	Veggie Salad & White Bean	Lettuce Wraps	Sweet & Savory Hummus Plate	Hummus & Veggie Sandwich	Lettuce Wraps
Dinner	Kale Frittata & Cauliflower	Soup of Vegan Carrot Ginger	Roasted Carrot Soup	Apple Soup & Curried Parsnip	Pumpkin Curry Soup	Golden Veggie Soup	Beef Balti & Lamb

Snack							
	Rice Cake Sandwich	Garlic Hummus	Chickpea Snack Salad	Mango-Date Energy Bites	Peanut Butter Energy Balls	Beet Jerky	Avocado Hummus
Salad, Dressing & Appetizer	Sweet Potato Salad	Greek Salmon Salad	Chicken & Wild Rice Soup	Jerk Tofu Grain Bowls	Spicy Salmon Bowl	Grilled Tomatoes	Honey Mustard Chicken

Conclusion

Hopefully after reading this cookbook, you have understood all about the anti-inflammatory diet. This cookbook emphasizes on the anti-inflammatory diet basics, the delicious easy to make recipes and many more.

Many modern diseases & disorders are triggered by chronic inflammation, & many people are hurt. If you're one of them, you realize how hard it is to get relief. Blood pressure, flow, diabetes, & other potentially deadly diseases are all worsened by inflammation in your body.

The biggest hurdle that prevents individuals from sticking with the proper foods is realizing what to eat & having the plan to accomplish. Now you've both tools at your disposal in this best cookbook. Whether you are looking to relieve pains, aches & headaches, abdominal irritation, fatigue, or mass loss, this cookbook will provide you with the superfoods to relieve your physique.

The values of anti-inflammatory food are yet very relevant today & have increasingly gained recognition over the last twenty years, as surveys continue to encourage the theory that food could reduce chronic inflammation & can reduce or stop the occurrence of chronic disease.

BONUS: scanning the following QRcode will take you to our Gdrive page where you can securely access and download our BONUS PDF. Enjoy it!

Made in United States
Troutdale, OR
06/06/2024